The King of Alsander by James Elroy Flecker

James Elroy Flecker was born on 5th November 1884, in Lewisham, London.

Flecker does not seem to have enjoyed academic study and achieved only a Third-Class Honours in Greats in 1906. This did not set him up for a job in either government service or the academic world.

After some frustrating forays at school teaching he attempted to join the Levant Consular Service and entered Cambridge to study for two years. After a poor first year he pushed forward in the second and achieved First-Class honours. His reward was a posting to Constantinople at the British consulate.

However, Flecker's poetry career was making better progress and he was beginning to garner praise for his poems including The Bridge of Fire. Unfortunately, he was also showing the first symptoms of contracting tuberculosis. Bouts of ill health were to now alternate with periods of physical well-being woven with mental euphoria and creativity.

Before his early death he managed to complete several volumes of poetry, which he continually revised, together with some prose works and plays. It was a small canon of work but on his death on 3rd January 1915, of tuberculosis, in Davos, Switzerland he was described as "unquestionably the greatest premature loss that English literature has suffered since the death of Keats".

DEDICATED To J.N. MAVROGORDATO

This Romance, of which he never despaired in the Rough
Is dedicated in the Ripe

Index of Contents
Preface
Chapter I—Blaindon
Chapter II—Alsander
Chapter III—En Pension in Alsander
Chapter IV—Introducing a good beggar and a bad King
Chapter V—Of the knighting of Norman Price
Chapter VI—Concerning Isis and Aphrodite: with a digression on the shocking treatment the latter's followers receive from the hands of English novelists
Chapter VII—The Society for the Advancement of Alsander
Chapter VIII—How Norman failed to pass a qualifying examination for the post of King of Alsander, and was whipped: together with a digression on the excellence of whipping
Chapter IX—The Consul
Chapter X—Contains the President's tale and a debate on the advantages of murder
Chapter XI—A Visit to Vorza
Chapter XII—In which the Beetles crawl
Chapter XIII—Re-Coronation
Chapter XIV—Princess Ianthe

Chapter XV—Peronella and the Priest
Chapter XVI—The Counter Conspiracy: an episode in the style of the worst writers
Chapter XVII—Battle
Chapter XVIII—The Poet visits Blaindon once more, and takes John Gaffekin to the seashore, where a miracle occurs
An Essay on James Elroy Flecker
James Elroy Flecker – A Short Biography
James Elroy Flecker – A Concise Bibliography

PREFACE

Here is a tale all romance—a tale such as only a Poet can write for you, O appreciative and generous Public—a tale of madmen, kings, scholars, grocers, consuls, and Jews: a tale with two heroines, both of an extreme and indescribable beauty: a tale of the South and of sunshine, wherein will be found disguises, mysteries, conspiracies, fights, at least one good whipping, and plenty of blood and love and absurdity: a very old sort of tale: a tale as joyously improbable as life itself.

But if I know you aright, appreciative and generous Public, you look for more than this in these tragic days of social unrest, and you will be most dissatisfied with my efforts to please you. For you a king is a shadow, a madman a person to be shut up, a scholar a fool, a grocer a tradesman, a consul an inferior grade of diplomatic officer, and a Jew a Jew. You will demand to know what panacea is preached in this novel as a sovran remedy for the dismal state of affairs in England. With what hope do I delude the groaning poor: with what sarcasm insult the insulting rich? What is the meaning of my apparent joyousness? What has grim iron-banging England to do with sunshine, dancing, adventure and, above all, with Poets?

In support of my reputation let me hasten to observe that in my efforts to please a generous and appreciative Public I have not failed to insert several passages of a high moral tone. Grave matters of ethics are frequently discussed in the course of my story, and the earnest inquirer may learn much from this book concerning the aim, purpose and origin of his existence. To Government and its problems I have given particular attention, and the observant reader may draw from these subtle pages a complete theory of the Fallacy of the Picturesque. Only I implore the public to forgive the Poet his proverbial licence, to remember that truth is still truth, though clad in harlequin raiment, and thought still thought, though hinted and not explained.

Farewell, then, my King of Alsander. Ride out into the world and conquer. Behind you—a merry and a mocking phantom—my youth rides out for ever!

Beyrouth, Syria, 1913.

THE KING OF ALSANDER

CHAPTER I

BLAINDON

*Would that I had a little cot
Beside a little hill,
In some romantic English spot
Where summer's not so very hot
And winter not too chill.*
J. Williams

The writer of these simple lines, now unhappily dead, was a man of the soil, whose sweet native note had never been troubled by the sinister depravities, the heartless affectations of urban existence; and I believe myself that his pathetic and modest ideal could have been actually realized had he inhabited, as perhaps he did, the peaceful village of Blaindon. This secluded hamlet lies some ten miles from the sea, in an undulating, but not terrible, country—a land of woodland and meadow, of buttercup and daisy, of tiny streams and verdant dells. At evening the scene is more tranquil than ever, and the old church spire, standing sentinel above the cold ploughlands, presents a curiously sad appearance, tinged as it is with the melancholy of years. However at the time when this story opens it was not evening, but afternoon, and a very hot one. The horse in his freedom, like the pig in his confinement, lolled upon the ground, and the thatches rustled with the melodies of sleep.

Yes, let us look beneath those thatches and consider the village yokel for a moment, as with mouth agape and heavy eyelids he takes his meed of repose:

Nec partem solido demere de die
Spernit; nunc viridi membra sub arbuto
Stratus; nunc ad aquae lene caput sacrae.

But if, here in England, he has no arbute tree, or sacred fountain, whereby to stretch his large, unwieldy limbs, there awaits him, nevertheless, the fireside in winter, the straw of the stable loft for hotter days. Ensconced beneath such lowly roofs as those of little Blaindon, many a hundred sons of toil have been born, been married and been finally dead, after a life spent in working nobly for an ignoble pittance, far away from the wearisome strife of new ideas and endeavours, and all the rumbling of the world's chariot wheels.

I have carefully examined the records in the parish church, thinking that they might interest all those who still have faith in the sterling qualities and bulldog tenacity of our British yeoman class. I discovered the interesting fact that only a fifth of the population die before the age of sixty-five; and that the same families seem to have lived here in a state of ceaseless intermarriage for century after century. The Weolkeðings of Saxon days, the Weilcans of the Normans, who are they but the honest Wilkinses round the corner? No great calamities have occurred at Blaindon except an occasional plague; no stirring battles have there been fought. The place seems to have been forgotten or overlooked during the Civil Wars. (However, an inhabitant of the town fought at Balaclava, but not in the Heavy Brigade.) Of the prevailing insanity, I need say nothing; this is the inheritance of all rustic communities. That the people of Blaindon are happy and appreciate their charming home they have proved in the clearest possible way. They have never left it.

Would that he who looks over the church-yard wall down at the tidy rows of one-room cottages, whose gardens blaze with nasturtia and red daisies, could say that no jarring note, no trace of a restless individuality, marred the enchanting scene. But, alas! every traveller is bound to remark a peculiarly ugly two-storied erection, whose rectangular bricks render it at once an eyesore and a solecism. This building used to be called by the inhabitants Price's bongmash: but the name on its sign was Bon Marché (French for Good Market). Mr Price's business was at the time this story opens the most flourishing concern in Blaindon. It was carried on chiefly by the indomitable energy of the younger Price; his father now slept most of the day, not so much on account of his advancing years as because he was very tired and a heavy eater. He could trust his son completely. Young Norman Price was one of the most envied personages in Blaindon. He was only nineteen; a handsome and strong young man, and the face he showed a customer wore no servile frock-coated smirk, but a laugh of real pleasure at being able to supply the needs of the community. Nearly everything was on sale in his shop—all groceries, also cloth, garden seeds, papers, books (the least flourishing part of the trade), and tobacco. Yet his store did not look at all like other village stores where everything is bought in dirty pennyworths. It was well arranged, and the goods were displayed to good account, more after the tradition, I fear, of American vulgarity than of British honesty. Worse still, Price had actually taken upon himself to corrupt the adorable simplicity of the villagers and to turn their thoughts to the enervating fashions of great cities. If a young villager came in who liked to be thought rather a nut and who fancied himself in a new waistcoat, the young grocer would give him a little elegant and expensive tobacco to try, explain that he smoked it himself, and that one smoked less of it than of the commoner sorts, so it came no dearer after all. He utterly refused to sell cigarettes at ten for a penny, or assorted sweets at three half-pence the quarter. It soon became a mark of distinction to be a customer at the Bon Marche, and the firm got a reputation for selling "sound articles and no trash."

I have not mentioned, however, the object that would probably most astonish a gentleman of culture on entering the shop. On the wall hung a large and fine reproduction of Holbein's portrait of Georg Gisze. The young merchant, robed in delicate silk and velvet, and surrounded by keys, quadrants, scissors, maps, and ledgers, was obviously meant to be the tutelary deity of the house; indeed, as a set-off to the flowers that stand upon the painted table, Norman had placed a large bowl of carnations on his counter.

The picture had been a present from his friend, John Gaffekin. If young Price appears in this story so strangely different from his father and from the other villagers of Blaindon, and indeed from all grocers whatsoever, we need not accept the explanation of some, that his father was "a deeper man than you'd think" or the assertion of others that he "got it from his mother," a lady of whom he had never seen so much as a photograph. The lad's singularity was much more likely due to this curious and close intimacy with a gentleman: and I hope that those who read this history will not close the book without a sigh of remonstrance against all those who insist on giving the lower classes thoughts above their station. John Gaffekin lived with his widowed mother in the Elizabethan Blaindon Hall, a typical old country house standing just outside the village on a plot of park. The old lady was infirm, and in order that he might attend to his mother, and also avoid drawing on a by no means unlimited income, John had never gone to school. He had taken some lessons from the Vicar, who had been "a fine classic in his day," and as he naturally loved books and was of a quiet disposition he became so proficient that the Reverend George Apple warmly urged him to try for a scholarship at Oxford. For a long time he had refused even to attempt this feat. He declared that he could not leave his mother. He feared he could not win the scholarship. But the old lady joined her importunities to those of the Vicar. "They had not enough money to go on for ever," she maintained, "and if John had a degree he would always be able to turn his hand to something at a pinch, and earn his daily bread." Very much at a pinch, had the dear old lady but known it!

"I can easily get some one to look after me," said the old lady, "and it is very wrong of me not to have sent you away before. You are getting buried in this stupid place, and too dreamy altogether, with no one here but that grocer friend of yours to talk to."

"I wish Norman could come with me to Oxford," said John. "It's wrong of me to leave him."

"My dear son, I can't have you consorting with that sort of person all your life."

"I do hate that subject," protested John.

"My dear boy, you'll find the wisdom of my words when you've seen a little more of the world," said Mrs Gaffekin.

"Besides," interposed the Vicar, tactfully, "College terms only account for half the year. We shall see plenty of you down here."

So John got his scholarship and went to Oxford, and Norman found himself rather lonely. One day, three years ago, John had begun to talk to him when he came into Blaindon to buy tobacco, and since then they had been continuously together, walking, fishing and shooting all over the place, and conversing on high and learned topics. That is why Norman was an educated man after a certain curious fashion. He was, however, no mere counterpart of his friend. Left to himself, Norman had fire and intelligence enough to make his mark. But the sudden wide prospect opened up by all that golden world all those enchanted gardens that lie hid between pasteboard covers—had dazzled his eyes and made him a most exceptional person. He had plunged into everything, learnt Latin and French, attempted Greek. There were very few books that he read carefully; hardly one would he read twice. "There are so many more to read," he used to say. No one could be less of a scholar, and the fine points of characterization, the delicate shades of metre and language, lay beyond his sphere. But he loved all the books that are not generally read; he could feel that such books were peculiarly his own property or his own discovery, and a habit of always reading books that no one else has read is not a bad guide to literature. All the works that glow with dark frenzy, or with diabolical Rembrandt fires, whose authors died nameless deaths or were burnt for magic, all the fantastic tales about new countries on the other side of mountains, or happy islands in limitless seas, all stories of the moon or stars were his especial delight and continual joy. For he loved the Monk of Monk Lewis, and this is a rare book to find, and Vathek, and William Jordan, Junior, greatest of unread modern books; and he sang to himself the Gods of Pegana and dreamed over its ethereal pictures, and he loved the new Irish tales. And he adored that mysterious wonder-story of the Golden Ass, and its glittering precious style; and he read Richepin's tales of the Roman decadence. And he never wearied of James Thompson (not of the "Seasons"), or of Baudelaire, or of the great travel poems of the world from the Odyssey to Waring.

And here, again, I must point the moral. The egregious bad taste of this young man was almost certainly the outcome of his low antecedents. Stale romanticism is embedded in the poorer classes. He liked his literature garish and vivid, and with his insistent passion for all the decadent stuff that used to be in favour ten or twelve years ago, he could never appreciate that really noble modern literature, much of it dramatic, which tackles so fearlessly and with such psychological insight the problems of our industrial age. In fact, he used to say that it might be damned good, but it was damned boring. Such is the obtuseness of the Philistine. He was, moreover, no critic, as you may well opine; he had not the fine taste of his friend, but he fell the more readily under the spell and domination of strange books; he was a dreamer, and entertained ideas of his own, which he would not have dared impart. Yet this dreamer was a man of business, and employed all the resources of a crude but powerful imagination in the disposal of his wares. How, then, could he help feeling a little weary of Blaindon, especially when John was away at Oxford? And on this afternoon, on which I have promised that my story should begin, he was sitting rather disconsolate in his shop, drowning care in the delights of Conrad's Youth.

He had hardly been interrupted the whole day, except for lunch. The sexton had been in for some twine, and the Vicar's daughter for some pink wool "to match the merino mother bought yesterday." She was a pretty girl, and Price almost aspired to marry her. Had he only known it, the poverty-stricken Mr Apple would have been only too glad, and I do not think the young lady was at all averse to Norman, whose beauty of person and brilliance of mind made one forget his unfortunate connexion with trade.

At about half-past three he shut the book with a bang, heaved a disconsolate sigh to think that the glorious tales were over, and stretched himself. Then he slid off the counter and looked down the high road to see if anything stirred thereon. Straight, broad, white, glaring, over the sleeping downs lay the deserted road that led to Blaindon from the unseen Ocean, fit for the trampling of armies and the shouting of men, a road for caravans and caravans of merchandise to traverse with bells a-jangle while wagoners told the tales of wagoners high perched on their creaking wains; yet a road for modern life, ready for tramways to glide along its hedges, and motor-cars to spin down its smooth and cambered way; yet perhaps chiefly an ancient road, down which some herald would speed, his gold coat laced with dust, his knees tight gripping his steaming horse, with a message of war, disaster, or relief. And down this mighty road came no wagon, nor army, nor motor, nor herald: no one save in the far distance a solitary walker, small and lonely in the vast sunshine. Price lazily watched the approaching figure. It seemed to be that of an old man, but if so this old man was walking faster than any other old man in the world. At all events, Price was already sure that he was no inhabitant of Blaindon, and he therefore came out and stood at his door to look at him.

It was indeed a tall, straight and singular old man who came up some twenty minutes later and halted opposite the Bon Marche, resting on his stick. His long hair and beard were of an almost dramatic whiteness, like those of a Father Christmas in sugar. What was seen of his face seemed smooth, and he had surprisingly young, blue eyes. Afterwards, one noticed his long archaic lips and the beauty of his hands. His clothes, subordinate as all clothes should be to the face, were yet curious and distinctive. He wore a mauve silk scarf, a sort of Norfolk jacket, a cricketing shirt, grey flannel trousers, and brown boots with pointed toes. No collar, and no hat. His stick was a stout partridge cane with a silver nameplate. The old man stood opposite Price and looked at him with fixed attention for at least half a minute.

"Have you got any Navy Cut, sir?" said the old man.

"Mild or medium?" said Norman, beating a retreat into the shop to let the stranger enter and to look for the tobacco.

"Strong, of course," bellowed the old man. "Thank you."

"What a voice he has!" thought the grocer. The new customer sat down on a chair and threaded out the tobacco into an enormous briar, looking curiously about him. Suddenly he started.

"You don't mean to say that you keep Menodoron Mixture here!" said he. "I haven't been able to get any in this damned county at all."

He tapped the Navy Cut out of his pipe, swept it into his pouch, and seized hold of the Menodoron tin. As he did so his eye lit upon the Holbein. He gave a second start, more violent than the first, a quick, violent spasm of his entire body, which made his snowy beard flap like the handle of a water pump.

"Hullo! Where did you get that from?"

"Georg Gisze? He's a present from a friend of mine."

"And all those books and dictionaries, are they for sale? Have you a Grammar School in this notable town?"

"No, sir. I read them when business is slack."

"Then what are you doing here?" said the old man, earnestly. "I can see you are not a gentleman: you look too much like a god. Tell me, what are you doing, with a library like that, here in a grocer's shop, in this horrible little village?"

"Now, come, sir," said Norman, "it's a picturesque old place, situated in charming country."

"Sir," replied the stranger, "I am a travelled man; I am perhaps a trifle over-proud of my great journeys. I have seen all the Great Effects. I have clambered among fearful crags to see the Euphrates, that old river, burst through the Gate of Taurus. I have seen the Alps from the Finsteraarhorn below me, Niagara from the footpath above me, night in the city, day in the desert, dawn on the sea. I have seen the Little Effects: Normandy, Tasmania, the English Lakes. But never on train, steamer, bicycle, tram, motor, balloon, camel, horse, mule, or foot, have I found such an unutterably dull place as Blaindon. Forgive this rhetoric, purveyor of sweetmeats, but be assured of its truth."

"In all places, sir, there is a sky, a sun, and stars."

"Where," pursued the stranger, "did you learn to talk with that pure accent, vendor of spices; or to frame such pleasant words? What are you doing in this fantastic shop?"

"Earning my living, sir. Nor is there any mystery about my case. I have a friend, now at Oxford, who gave me books to read and taught me Latin."

"Are you contented? Perfectly happy in your sunlight and starlight? Supremely satisfied with Catullus on the counter?"

"As a rule, yes. But my friend is away at present; there is no one to talk to, and these wonderful stories" (he pointed to the book lying face downward on the counter) "stir the soul to travel."

"Well, why not travel, O Lord of Things in Tins? Blaindon's no good for a man like you, great enough to make castles out of his biscuit tins, and fortifications out of washing soap." And he pointed to Norman's window, which was dressed that day with certain architectural effects.

"I have been content with my dreams for a long time," said Norman, with a little vulgar pride in his poetic and pathetic phraseology "I am fond of dreams—they are my best friends."

"If you imagine I am going to be impressed by that sort of Watts-Dunton talk you are wrong; I'm going," said the old man, as he pose up from his chair.

"Sir!" cried Norman; "you haven't paid for the tobacco."

The old man sat down with a thump.

"I am a poet," he said, with deprecatory grandeur. "And you aren't a cultured snob after all, but something of a man. Have you travelled at all, now? Tell me."

"Oh, yes, I go round the county a bit. On market days I usually go over to Iffcombe in the Marsh; it's quite lively there."

"By the Queen of the Moon and the Sea whom I worship and by the memory of your mother whom I swear you have never known, how dare you stand opposite me, a young man with the face of a god, and blither about Iffcombe in the Marsh! Travel, man, over the water, down south among the palms! You've got money?"

"Not I!"

"A little, surely!"

"Only about a hundred pounds of my own, so far."

"Only a hundred pounds! Then go away with it before your friend borrows it off you to pay his Oxford bills. No, don't get wrathful; I'm an Oxford man myself and understand that curious world. A hundred pounds! Why, I've never had a hundred pounds all at one time for many a year. How you can keep a hundred pounds in your pocket or in the bank, I do not know, when five pounds will take you to the Alps, seven to Italy, twelve to the Gulf of Corinth, thirty to Damascus,[1] and fifty to Yokohama. You should clear out of this rat-hole, young man, and that immediately. Why not to-night? as thundering Salvationists cry, desiring to save the soul. That engagement, this duty, the other promise, este, ese, aquel, as the Spaniards have it, leave it all and save your life, this is the Poet's appeal, the Muse's command. You'll find a kingdom somewhere, or a war, or an adventure. I am a prophet, and the worshipper of a Holy Lady. Now, good-bye."

He laid his hands on the boy's shoulders, and looked at him dramatically. Then he turned round, seized the tin of Menodoron and strode away.

"Two and sixpence," said Norman, calling him back.

"Two and elevenpence, counting the Navy Cut," said the poet, handing over the exact sum. "You will certainly succeed, Mr Norman Price. So I will give you a good tip," he added in a stage whisper. "Go straight to Alsander."

"Where's that?" said Norman, but the eccentric customer, without another word, strode out of the shop, leaving him bewildered. There was nothing to do in the shop; he tried to re-arrange some shelves, but felt it was not worth the trouble. He opened the Golden Ass and found he could not progress without looking up many exotic words, and the dictionary was too heavy. Finally he sat down on his counter, gazing at the sunswept fields and lengthening shadows of the hedges. The vast mournful light of the late afternoon penetrated his spirit, and he felt, not for the first time, that unutterable sadness, that vague and restless longing for the Unknown land Impossible that it is the privilege of young men to feel. For many a youth this curious sense of unity with the earth is but a first awakening of amorous desire, and to such a one Venus comes quickly, with all her gentle pain. But there are a few who understand their souls, or who have souls to understand, whose daydreams are fashioned of other delights and different imaginings.

So Norman began dreaming, at first as schoolboys dream of adventure, plot, swordsmanship, hidden treasures, dense jungles, heroic bravery, desperate efficiency and lost princesses. Then a poet's dream of hot suns, and open plains, and vast masses of swaying colour. Then he bethought himself of a multitude of pleasant practical schemes. John and he had often talked of a bicycling tour in Normandy. That would be inexpensive, but now it seemed so tame an affair. What of this delicately—named Alsander the Poet talked of? It sounded remote enough. To go somewhere where no one else had ever been would be better than reading books no one else had ever read. And one should go at an hour's notice, without making any plans. What a curiously-inspired man this old poet or artist was! Quite mad, no doubt, with his Holy Lady. And what did he mean by mentioning Norman's mother? Norman had no gods; he feared Death and loved Life. Well, since Life is short, and since one is sure of nothing, shall one not be bold? To-night!

The old man's words thrilled him. If, as the poet had suggested, a trumpet-voiced vulgarian in black can save a drinker from dirt and disease in a quarter of an hour, cannot a radiant poet save a dreamer from stagnation in ten minutes? Norman began to think hard, and his pulses were stirring for action, when the bell rang behind the shop. It was time for meat-tea.

Norman, with no feeling of any bathos, entered the parlour with the full intention of eating a hearty meal. He sat down opposite old William Price and began to cut himself enormous slices of bread. Meanwhile he looked at his father, and studied the old man's appearance carefully and cynically for the first time in his life. We often take some of our near relations for granted (like the nursery cuckoo clock or the cabbage-roses on the porch), and we never become acutely conscious of their existence or individuality unless they die, disappear, or make themselves offensive. Norman dispassionately scrutinized his father's stumpy red beard, curious veiled eyes, and fireless, thin face, remembered his equanimity and his shrewdness, and wondered with boyish shallowness and conceit—for he knew less about his father than about the man in the moon—what on earth he had in common with such a man outside human nature and the grocery business. The only recent change that Norman could observe in his parent was that he had certainly become fatter and more foolish since he had left his son to do all the grocery work. The lad was sure that the one salvation for his father would be to take the business on again, and his idea of effecting a dramatic departure—for a time, at least—grew almost a resolve.

Usually Norman never told his father anything that could possibly puzzle or worry the excellent old gentleman, and had maintained the rule that the elder generation is the last place where the new should expect sympathy. However, for want of something to talk about, Norman observed that a most peculiar person, describing himself as a poet, had been in the shop and had tried to persuade him to travel.

"To travel, eh?" said William Price. "What in?"

"Oh, he meant abroad."

"I've n'er bin abroa'," said the honest old fellow, stifling his words in large mouthfuls of ham. "But I bin 'sfuras Wales."

"I'm longing to go," said Norman, "and I will go, too."

"Ah, yes," said the old man, paying no serious attention, as he leaned back in his wooden armchair. "I've often wanted to see it myself. Used to live down by the sea in Kent, and I was always wunnering what was the other side, and thinking I saw France, but it was only the clouds. I'm glad I never went there though; they say it's a very irreligious country."

Norman finished his meal in silence and folded up his napkin.

"Good night, father," he said, as he got up from his chair, leaving the old man still hard at work. "I expect you'll want to get to sleep now, it's been a tiring day."

"Indeed it has," said William Price. "Indeed it has."

"I'm going out for a stroll," said Norman, at the door.

"Oh, we understand," gurgled Mr William Price after him, with a wink. "Young rip!" he added complacently as he continued his meal.

But when, his meal finished, he began to doze in the armchair by the fire, even his confident son might have been startled to see him open his wide dark eyes, unfilmed, and smile as though he saw Paradise dawn upon the ceiling.

Norman walked up and down the village street, as though he hoped that the moon, Whose silver bow hung listlessly above, would send some barbed messenger of watery fire to confirm him in a resolution. Whether indeed the celestial lady did touch him somehow, or whether his vanity and naughty desire to startle the villagers was not more powerful, cannot say; but in a few minutes a strange decided mood swept over him, and when a quarter of an hour later he swung into the Blaindon Arms it was as a man resolved to say good-bye.

For neither business nor inclination had ever permitted Norman to lose touch with these heroes of the soil, the Blaindon working class. They were honest, strenuous, interesting fellows, a little too full perhaps of local colour, Though they were a little jealous of him, they were a kindly folk and bowed naturally to his superior wealth. Superior intellect they did not allow him to possess. For them he was a bright boy who'd got "notions."

He greeted little Nancy at the bar as a habitué should, and asked for the time-table.

"Surely ye aren't goin' anywhere this tame o' nate," murmured John Oggs.

"Yes, I am," said Norman. "I'm just off abroad. And I've come to say good-bye."

"What!" said old Canthrop, a person who combined the functions of village patriarch and village imbecile, and was, in accordance with the universal custom of savage communities, almost worshipped in consequence. "What!" he repeated, making the mono-syllable rhyme with hat. "Aiy didn't know: no one tould me!"

"Well, you're the first to know as usual, Mr Canthrop. The old man doesn't know yet."

"What!" said old Canthrop, almost shrieking, "not tould yer feyther? Not tould yer feyther that yer goin' away?"

He rocked convulsively in his chair.

"Isn't that rather sudden of you, Mr Price?" said pleasant Nancy, simpering. She was a great friend of Norman's, and her voice was a little tremulous as she asked her question.

Thomas Bodkin, the sexton, who passed for a man of the world, and was drinking airily at the bar, leaned over and whispered very audibly, "It's a scrape, Nancy ... these young dogs ... must let 'em sow their oats ... eh, what?... We know."

Mr Bodkin's jerky mouthfuls passed in the inn for nimble elocution, his metaphors for the delicious slang of an old and experienced rake.

"Gawd!" ejaculated John Oggs, who was sitting behind him, "ye have it there, man, ye have it there!"

"What nonsense!" said Norman. "You don't imagine I should run away from trouble, do you? Or that I should be likely to get into trouble? Or that if I did I should be such a fool as to tell you anything about it?"

"Why did you, then?" said Thomas Bodkin. A roar of laughter greeted this vivacious sally.

Price looked round with rather priggish disgust. It was more than he could stand, this asinine mockery. "I came to say good-bye," he said.

"Till to-morrow, eh?" said the sexton. "You will not see me to-morrow," said Norman.

"See now, Mr Price," pursued the sexton, "there are no more trains. None between five this evening and 10.30 to-morrow, except on markets when the 8.15 goes to Iffcombe. You're mad."

Another peal of laughter, during which Norman disappeared, a baffled Byron, punished by the native humour of honourable working men for trying to produce a cheap effect.

But his resolution had received its final confirmation. He could not face the ridicule of the morrow. He hurried back at once to the shop, and there on the counter wrote a concise note to his father. He thought it unnecessary to condole or excuse. He knew how delightful it would be for the old man to have anything happen to him at all, how he would enjoy being the centre of sympathetic interest in the village, and how thoroughly good it would be for his moral character to get back to business. He then took the Post Office Savings Bank book from the safe. There were ninety pounds odd in it, entered in his name, the profits that had accrued during his two years' management of the shop. Perhaps it was not strictly his; his father had established the business, and provided the initial stock. But then his father had laid by enough to keep him even in food for the next ten years, and Norman had done the work. It is the young who want money; Norman had never been able to see the object of saving money with immense toil over against the day when one should become infirm, insane, or dead. He uttered a vigorous oath against the Post Office system, which means a day's delay in withdrawal, sent the book up to headquarters at once, asking that it should be sent him by return to the Central Post Office, Southampton, posted it in the box opposite, and then considered what he ought to pack. He took a change of raiment, and then looked lovingly at the ponderous tomes on his shelves. Only the smallest could go with him.

"After all," said Norman, "I have read all these once. New lands, new books, and I am not going away for what John would call a reading party."

Finally he took no book with him save a little Elzevir Apuleius, and packed it with all his other effects on his bicycle carrier and in the saddle-bag. Just as he was mounting one more thought troubled him. Would he not be terribly lonely? If only John could come too! "No," he said, arguing to himself, "my life must not consist of John. If I'm lonely I shall have to discover for myself new companions in new countries."

It was a splendid night. He set off down the High Street, on the main road to Southampton in a state of perilous exultation. Smoothly and quickly the tyred wheels bore him on out to infinity. The door of the Blaindon Arms stood open, and as he rolled noiselessly by he could hear Canthrop summing up his view of the situation for the fiftieth time,

"Bloody silly, I call it," said the old man, "bloody silly!"

[1] I should subjoin a word to prevent any enthusiastic reader from taking the words of the old poet too seriously and wasting thirty pounds in going to Damascus. It is a very filthy town with electric trams and no drains.

The fares mentioned by the poet are of course third-class.

CHAPTER II

ALSANDER

Know'st thou the land where bloom the lemon trees,
And darkly gleam the golden oranges?
A gentle wind blows down from that blue sky....

With a spear of golden light and gradual splendour Dawn rose on her triumphal car. In winter men rise up to welcome her advent: wives cast off sleep and light fires in her honour; the good citizens draw the curtains to gaze out upon her beauty, stretching their lazy limbs. In winter Dawn arises to the sound of chattering and bustle, the herald of man's work in town and field. But in summer only the grey mists and the light-winged birds listen to her as she rings the bells of day.

Norman had seen new lands and cities, and had been wandering on foot for many weeks to south and east admiring all things, but never so satisfied with what he saw as to rest for a single day. At the first glimmer of light he leapt to his window, and whether Dawn rose broken upon the peaks or solemn on the plain, whether she wandered mysteriously down old winding streets, or set the city square clattering and clanging, it was early, ever early, that our heroic traveller left his mean abode to seek the unexpressed, unknown, ever-receding city of his heart's desire.

One night as he was trudging along he met a tramp, whose face he could hardly make out beneath the stars, who, learning that he was bound to Alsander, talked to him in English passionately of the beauties of that country, recommended him to learn its language, and then disappeared into the gloom. This confirmed the boy in his definite aim, and day after day he approached this certain goal, fired by the eloquence of the mysterious stranger. This night, being among the high mountains, he had found no inn; however, undaunted, he lay down on the roadside for an hour or two, then rose and strode on, pack on shoulder, through the shadows. Who could be tired of walking with the mountain wind ahead, the dim white road beneath, and the joy of watching for the dawn! "Ah!" he thought, "how I pity the six-legged at their desks! What for them is the sunrise curtain to the drama of a day? How indeed should they greet it, save with a cry of pain and a curse upon the light? But I will wander on."

Now had come that shining moment of Eternity when Aurora unravels the folds of her saffron robe across the sky and bares her wounded breast to the blue of morning. The boy swung round a corner of the highway, and suddenly beheld the valley far below. He saw quiet forests of tall golden trees and meadows so rich with gentian and wild pansy that even at that far height he could see them shine. To his left, at the edge of the plain, lay spear-sharp mountains, a little darker than the skies, whose distant hollows and tortuous cones ever hinted at the mystery of the next valley and the joy of things unseen. He saw the thin torrent which tumbled down in cascades behind the wall become a quiet and solemn river below leading to a curved strip of sea, of an intense unearthly colour, southern, fantastic, beyond all belief, and the sound of rushing waters seemed the only sound in the world. But most surprising of all, on a rocky mound between the mountains and the bay rose the white city of Alsander, with her legendary towers and red roofs all dreaming in the sunlight. In such deep slumber lay that perfect city, the boy held the very sight of it to be a dream. For there surely dwelt the good King and the bad King, the younger son and the three princesses, the dwarf, the giant and the gnome. Surely in those blue mountains lurked and lolled the devastating dragon who came down for his yearly toll of maiden flesh; surely in that blue sea swam all the shoal of nereids and dolphinous fishy beings whose song is dangerous to men. Thus appeared the city of Alsander to Norman as he gazed at it over the wall in silence. "Blessings on the head of that wonderful old tramp," said Norman, "who told me Alsander was the loveliest place in Europe and directed my steps on this glorious path; wherever he may be may joy attend him, so boldly did he bear the weight of years." Then down he went on his way again, humming to himself,

"Knowst thou the land where bloom the lemon trees?"

and the birds were frightened of his deep voice and the little green lizards fled up the walls as he strode on down the hill.

Many men can only enjoy beauty when they face it alone. These dark and solitary aesthetes love to ramble on the most horrible downs and heaths at intempestival morning hours, drinking in the miserable and fearsome aspect of the world. One such has said to me that he would walk half a day to avoid meeting a friend. I fear, too, that these characters consider their misanthropic tastes a self-evident mark of their superiority over the mass of men, who, herding together with vivacious chatter, much love-making, and explosion of corks, crowd to the prettiest places they know to enjoy Bank Holiday. Your lonely man claims a special communion with God or with the Spirit of Nature, or with the Rosicrucian mysteries of his own soul, so that his ramble becomes a sacrament, purifying by pity, terror and love. Norman was a little above this sort of rubbish: he felt dimly the cruelty of beauty and the menace of solitude. This sent him moving and set him longing—longing very definitely for human companionship. Thus he fell short of the self-sufficient man recommended by Aristotle, for which the reader may devoutly praise the Lord.

But the stilted style of this century can ill express the fluctuations of our hero's feelings. "Who is there" (I should have written in 1820), "or what man of feeling and imagination can be found, who, upon contemplating the ineffable grandeur and unspeakable majesty of Nature, does not ardently aspire to hold at the same moment communion with some divinely tender female heart, to read in those liquid eyes his own reflections purged of their dross and transmuted into gold, to press those sensitive fingers and thereby lose himself in rapture among the gorgeous scenes that astonish and confound his gaze, to seal those fluttering lips with the memory of an unforgettable moment?"

To resume the use of the English language, Norman felt lonely, and for that very reason paid particular attention to the only figures discernible in the landscape. He came down and the figures came up, three companions they seemed to be. But presently Norman made out that the central figure was a girl, and her two shining companions were only the two pails she carried, slung from a yoke that passed behind her neck. "Life for me," said Norman to himself, as he and the girl drew near to each other at the combined rate of six miles an hour, "is crude marble, and I have come here to carve it into flowers, and the flowers of youth are the fairest of them all." Pleased with this ingenuous comparison, he looked up with a smile, and discovered that the neck which bore the yoke was a shapely one, and that there in front of him, not fifty yards away, stood a young girl, with her pails clanking at her side. She was dressed in a white frock and her head was covered with a white kerchief edged with gold.

The reader now dreads the inevitable love scene, and I, too, feel that an apology is needed. For so many novelists, ballad-makers, jongleurs, troubadours, minstrels, poets, and bards have sung the praises of perfect, adorable and captivating ladies that I am inclined to lament with one of them that

I have sung all love's great songs
And have no new songs to sing,
But I'll sing the old songs again.

And so I will. We will have those old songs again, for I will not give my heroine "plain but interesting features" or "a noble rather than beautiful countenance with intellect shining in her eyes," or even in a candid moment declare her to possess "a haunting plainness all her own." But apart from all this there is the truth to consider, and this young girl was assuredly one of the most perfect women God ever made by accident or Satan by design.

For she stood there in front of him in the radiant, dancing, dewy morning, happy and unperturbed, in her gracious half-human beauty, not majestic, not passionate, not mysterious, but unreal from her very loveliness, a nymph, not of the woods or rivers, but of the sea—yet not of the tempestuous main—no tall sad siren of a treacherous rock, but a sweet, young pleasant nymph from a bay where the sun is always shining, a sea-sand nymph not unacquainted with flowers.

For when I would deal with her face and body, all those feeble, pretty comparisons whereby the pen of the writer strives to emulate the brush of the painter, must be of the sea or of flowers. Her dark hair, fringed against the gold lace of her scarf—but those same painters (whom all we word-workers envy bitterly but dare not say so) have shown how many confluent colours—hyacinth and blue and red and deep red gold, gleam in the shadowy hollows of the hair we fools call dark. ... Dark! As the sea-water in a sunlit bay lies dark between two little island rocks yet ripples in the wind, and the sea flowers turn it red along the marge and the depths glow violet in the midst, and the sunshine is all near but hidden—am I not now describing the dark hair of a lovely woman?

"But her eyes, poor poet, her eyes—are they not also pools of the salt sea?"

Not the eyes of this lass, my gentle friend. Her eyes were of finer and subtler essence than the heavy water of the sea. They were blue—which is ever most wonderful with dark lashes, dark brows and sea-dark hair—but not the dark blue of a rock pool nor yet quite the light broken blue of the blinking waves in the calm and brilliant bay. Her eyes were of a light dry fire—the blue not of sea nor of sky, but rather of the glowing air that swims about the idle fisher's boat hour after hour on summer days. So that you could not tell if they were deep eyes or light wayward eyes,—those little gay discs of laughing sunlit air.

And her countenance, that was a sweet rose and jasmine garden—but always, I would have you remember, a garden that blossoms by the sea, with vistas of the bay down every alley of the roses, and gleams of blue water glinting behind the trellis of the jasmine, and the sea air slightly touching the colour of all the flowers. Have you not seen the flowers in that Italian picture that are flung round Venus as she rises from the sea! Even so a little paler than the brave inland flowers were the jasmine and roses in the garden of the countenance of this lovely girl.

And her body? Can I tell you its secret? Ah, never: but as you leave the garden—pluck one tendril from the vine.

Her light, gracious, flowing beauty trans-ported the boy to the days he had read of, the days when the world was young. The chains of commerce and the shackles of class,—as it were, the last tatters of his black British clothes—fell from him. Looking at her, he smiled.

She evidently took that smile as a greeting intended for her, for she seemed to wait for him to come down and to be in no hurry with her pails.

"Good morning," she cried to him as he approached, in the honeyed and somewhat languorous speech of Alsander.

"Good morning," said Norman. "May I help you with the water?" Alsandrian is an easy, simple, and sonorous language, and Norman had been learning it and talking it to himself ever since the tramp he met in the night had directed his thoughts and footsteps toward the country of Alsander, yet he was very shy at practising for the first time this newly-acquired tongue.

"Ah, I thought you were a foreigner," said the girl, speaking with the strained simplicity and slight mispronunciation that we all of us employ for the benefit of strangers and infants. "What is your country and your home?"

"England."

"England? Why you are the first Englishman I have ever seen! How beautiful you are!"

Norman smiled, unable, and indeed unwilling, to deprecate his personal appearance.

"It is you who are beautiful," he said, slowly, labouring with the strange tongue, "Are they all like you in Alsander?"

"Do you think it possible?"

She drew herself up with such grace that Norman's arms twitched and ached. But he was rather in awe of her.

"How bright your eyes are!" he said.

"Are they? What colour do you think they are?" she asked, turning them full on him.

"They are blue. I have never seen such blue eyes in my life before."

"You are quite sure that they are not green?"

Norman was not at all sure that they were not: they seemed to him to change colour like little bright clouds, and shone at that moment like a lustrous emerald. But he simply said that they were not green, as he could only make very simple phrases in the language of Alsander.

"Are you going to stay long in this country?" inquired the girl.

"I think I shall have to."

He carved a dust pattern with his stick quite nervously, daring no more to look at her eyes. He asked her name.

"Peronella," she said. "And yours?"

"My name is Norman."

"Nor-mano, how nice!" said the girl, who seemed to think that this bashful northerner needed encouragement. "Normano. I shall always call you Normano."

"Always?" said Norman, looking up quickly.

The shameless maiden hung her head with a rosy blush as though she had been caught in an indiscretion,—as though the word had slipped from her unawares. But even at six in the morning, a sane though splendid hour, Norman, that reserved young Englishman, considered such encouragement sufficient. He went deliberately and took the pails off the girl's shoulders, as though he were going to help her, and the moment they had clattered on the road, he embraced this adorable girl from behind and kissed her ravenously. The kiss fell some two inches below her left ear.

She stood very stiff, flushed and angry; but Norman simply maintained his pressure till her whole body unstiffened. Norman had adopted to good purpose the principle that returns the penny-in-the-grip machine and secures for Britain her extensive Empire.

By this time they had become thoroughly nervous of each other. They sat down side by side on the wall near the spring. Norman ruffled his hair in embarrassment. Peronella murmured something about Fate. Norman inwardly disagreed; he did not think he ought to blame (or thank) Fate for the present contingency.

"Where are you going to stay?" asked the girl at last.

"As near you as possible."

"But don't you really know?"

"I know nothing. I am just a stranger, and I have come here for a ... for a ... damn," said Norman in English to himself, "what's the word for a holiday?—for a rest."

"You don't look as if you wanted a rest, and you won't get it if you stay near me."

"Not rest," said Norman, "not rest exactly, but ... amusement. O Peronella, you know how hard it is to talk a foreign tongue. I have learnt Alsandrian in a book, but I have never talked a word of it before."

"You talk it very nicely indeed; it is charming to hear you. It is not at all pleasant for us to hear men from Ulmreich talking Alsandrian. They make a horrible harsh noise, although they talk very carefully. But I think the lazy way you pronounce your o's and e's is charming...."

"I think," said Norman, looking at his watch with a smile, "that it is just twenty minutes since I first saw you and already...."

"Well?"

"I love you very much." He meant only to say "I like you very much," but in southern lands the linguistic distinction does not exist.

The girl seized him by the wrists.

"Don't say things like that, you devil," she cried, "especially if you do not mean it. Yes, say it even if you do not mean it; I love to hear you saying it. But be very careful. We are not like heathen women."

"I mean it!" said Norman, perforce.

"Normano, did you treat all other girls like this in England, and do you think I allow other men...."

"It will be quite different," faltered Norman.

"Say it again!"

"Peronella, I really love you."

Norman could not conceal a little yawn in his voice even at the moment of making this startling declaration; his eyes were heavy with light and he had walked for many hours. The girl perceived at once.

"Why, you are quite tired!" she said, "and talking fearful nonsense. You must come and find a room at once. Have you been walking long?"

"Four or five hours," said Norman.

"You curious person, to go walking in the night. Where have you come from?"

"From Braxea. I had my supper in the inn last night, and I've been walking ever since."

"What a pace you must have put on! Why, it's ever such a way away. Braxea? Why, it's right over the mountains on the frontier. Those long legs!" she added, pointing to them with a laugh. "No wonder they go far. I have never seen such long legs, except on a grass-hopper. And now you will walk into Alsander. But you have not yet answered my question. Where are you going to stay in our city?"

"I don't know a bit, beautiful girl, as I told you. Perhaps you can find me a place, not far away from you."

"Ah, perhaps I might," said she, "and perhaps I might not. I do not think you would be an agreeable neighbour."

"Ah, why not? Should I trouble and annoy you?"

"You have no idea how to behave, none at all," murmured Peronella.

"Oh, I will learn," cried the boy, "if you will teach me."

"And you will promise never, never again to squeeze my breath out in that awful manner?"

"Faithfully I will promise everything you ask."

"Why, then," said Peronella, rising up, with her eyes sparkling, "you had better come and live with my mother and me. We have a little pension and we want a lodger."

"What?" said Norman, not trusting himself to have understood.

"Come—and—live—with—my—mother-and—me, that is, if you like."

"O Peronella, I am afraid." And indeed the boy was really getting seriously frightened of this persistent maiden.

"But will you come? Or will you not have enough rest or amusement? Perhaps you would rather stay at the Palace Hotel. Most foreigners do. Ours is a very poor house. But the Palace Hotel is not really a palace. Will you come? It would be much less expensive for you, and we have no mosquitoes, and mother cooks divinely."

"How dare you ask me, you mad girl? You must think we live in snow houses and get our hearts frozen up in the north. Let us go at once!"

He made as if to accompany her, highly pleased at his proficiency in Alsandrian.

"No, no," said the girl. "That will never do. People are beginning to get up now and would say all sorts of things. You do not know what tongues they have, the old women of the town. I should be shamed and ruined. But I have a beautiful plan. You must walk about thirty yards behind me and follow me home."

Norman shook his head at her, not understanding. It is so much easier to be metaphorical than to be practical in a foreign tongue.

If you do not understand what I mean, consider a moment. You possess, let us say, a little knowledge of Italian, without tears. You are in a restaurant at Rome, and two Counts are discussing at the next table. To your delight you comprehend them perfectly. The Count with the white imperial has just observed, "La vera educazione, il segreto del progresso umano, e ideale." You admire the limpidity of his thought, the purity of his enunciation, and your own knowledge of a tongue so recently acquired. Then comes the infernal waiter with his coarse, plebeian accent. Where are you now? Minestra, cipolle, rombo, sermone—is the old Count going to preach one? Holding back the scalding tears of shame, you feed the brute with English.

Norman's obtuseness dismayed the girl.

"Oh, dear!" said she. "You don't understand a word. You are dreadfully stupid. What shall I do? Ah, I know!"

Laughing merrily, she picked up two pebbles, one longer than the other.

"You," she said, "and me."

Then she thrust Norman's stick into the grass to represent home, she explained. Then, kneeling down and pulling Norman beside her, she made the pebbles walk after her at even distances towards the stick. She made the short pebble trip along lightly with a mincing gait, while the tall one paced behind in gigantic strides, reverent and slow. At the stick she put another great pebble, squat and dumpy, to do duty for Mamma. The lady pebble tapped at the door and was admitted; the tall pebble thumped a few minutes afterwards; it talked inquiringly to the dumpy pebble, bowed to the graceful pebble, and finally (so Norman contrived to the girl's vast delight) kissed that graceful pebble rapturously behind the squat one's back.

"Now," said she, "do you understand, you stupid?"

Norman understood the little pantomime. She started off. He had to call her back for her forgotten pails. Norman filled them and placed them lovingly on her back. She went a full hundred yards ahead, and then waved her hand, nearly spilling her pails as she did so. He followed, rather frightened, very thrilled, and overwhelmingly tired.

Not otherwise did the Ithacan follow Nausicaa into the city of the Phoeacians whose ships went wisely in the waves.

CHAPTER III

EN PENSION IN ALSANDER

You, sweet, have the power
To make me passionate as an April day;
Now smile, then weep; now pale, then crimson red;
You are the powerful moon of my blood's sea.
The Witch of Edmonton

Norman followed, through the crumbling gateway, past an old fountain half buried in roses, up narrow tortuous ways at the back of a huge cathedral. Then he came to a street of steps. The town was beginning to awake. Little boys and girls had begun to play on the thresholds with portentous solemnity; half-naked men were washing their brown bodies at the pumps; and from the newly opened shutters many a glittering eye marvelled at the fair-haired stranger, as though he were some adventurous prince from the fantastic North, where it snows one half the year and rains the other, and red devils dance and moan in the perpetual fog.

Norman saw Peronella disappear inside a house in the distance; he came up to it and entered. The staircase was a long one, and there were innumerable doors. However, he proceeded up the very dirty steps as long as the splashings from the pail guided him onwards. "She cannot have much water left in that pail," thought Norman. At last the splashing ceased by a door whereon hung the notice:

"VIDVINO PRASKO
CAMBRI PRO LUI,"

signifying, as even Norman apprehended, that the lady of the house, a widow, would let rooms. Behind the door he heard Peronella chattering with exaggerated vigour. He rang, and the girl opened, scanned him up and down with mild astonishment (a piece of delicate acting, for which there was no reason whatever, as her mother, the widow Prasko, was busy clanking pans in the kitchen), and asked him what he wanted.

"I want to live here in a room," was the muddled reply.

"Wait a minute then, sir; I will speak to mother about it."

She shut the door in his face with a crashing slam, and ran into the kitchen.

"Mother," she said, in an impartial voice, as soon as there was a lull in the clanking of the kettles, "here is a foreign gentleman wanting a room."

"An Ulmreicher?"

"I don't know where he comes from; but I am sure he is not from Ulmreich."

"Because, you know," said the old lady, "however poor we may be, I could not stand having one of those people in the house: I simply hate them. They want all the floors cleaned with petroleum every day, and if there's a flea in the bed they curse one as if one were a beggar. It's no good, Peronella. I don't want any foreigners here, male or female. I never met a foreigner who was not much more interested in the way his room was dusted than in the style his food was cooked. Tell him to go away."

"You had really better look at him first, mother. He looks such a very nice foreigner, and not a bit like an Ulmreicher. And though he is very dusty, I noticed he had a gold watch chain."

"Well, well, girl, wait a bit and I'll come and see him. But I won't have one of those dirty Ulmreich pigs coming here and fussing about the fleas."

Norman, waiting outside the door, heard, even understood, the widow's remarks, for she nearly always spoke at the top of her voice, and invariably acted on the assumption, usually justifiable, that no foreigner could speak more than three words of Alsandrian. Yet he observed that the old lady's screech was not altogether unpleasant; it was, at all events, a peculiarly powerful noise. When the widow at length appeared at the door, a gigantesque apparition, he felt her to be striking enough to have a superior voice, or even to be the mother of Peronella. True, her face was wrinkled like an old lemon, or like a raised map of some uncharted country on the invisible side of the moon; and the vast cylinder of blue apron that she wore was not calculated to palliate either the rugosity of her face or the extreme fatness of her body. Yet for all her monstrous appearance she walked well, and had regular features, which suggested that neither her intelligence nor her will had disappeared, and had once been wedded to beauty.

"Do you come from Ulmreich?" she said to Norman in the language of that country, scanning him up and down.

Norman, though he knew enough Ulmreichan to master the import of her question, pretended not to understand, and stood dumb.

"Where do you come from?" the widow pursued in Alsandrian.

"From England."

"Ah, from England. I never knew anyone from England, but when I was in Ulmreich I met an American whose name I have forgotten, but he was a nice man, in a good line of business, till he died. And how long have you been in Alsander?"

"I have only just arrived."

"You have only just arrived. And you talk the language?"

"I learnt it on my way."

"And how did you find out my house, if you have only just arrived? We do not advertise: we are not a regular pension. Only it happens we sometimes let a room."

"I was wandering round looking for a room, and some one directed me here."

"Now who could that be?"

"Oh, I don't know. A little man round the corner."

"I wonder who it was. Was it a little cobbler with red hair? That would be Simone. Did you notice if he had red hair?"

"I don't know," said Norman, inwardly consigning the old girl to perdition. "He wore a felt hat."

"Ah, Simone has no hat," said the Widow Prasko. "And have you any luggage?"

"It is coming on by train."

"Did you not come by train yourself?"

"No," said Norman, crossly. "I have walked all night, from Braxea, and I am very tired. Please give me a room or refuse a room and send me away, at once."

"Ah, forgive me," said the widow, quite courteously, "but I have a daughter in the house, and I must ask questions. And, of course, you must be either very mad or very poor or you would not have walked from Braxea, and if you had walked you would have gone to the hotel."

"Do I look like the sort of man who would misbehave with your daughter?" said Norman, stiffly.

"Oh, I don't mind how you behave with per. But you might want to marry her, and I should not like her to marry a poor man."

"I am fairly rich," said Norman, "but I have not seen your daughter long enough to decide about marriage."

"You are rich and you want to find a room here?"

"Yes, please."

"And food?"

"Yes, food, too."

"You will find it rather simple living. You would live much better at the hotel."

"I would rather be here," said Norman. "I like to have people to talk to; I do not like hotels."

"Well, you might as well come in and see the room."

She showed him a small bedroom, almost entirely filled by an enormous curtained bed. It was a pretty room, papered in pale blue, ornamented with cuttings from French illustrated papers, a statuette of a nakedish lady apparently eight feet high, called Mignon, an oleograph representing a romantic northern castle surrounded by impossible waterfalls, and a clock which had been for many years too tired to work. Peronella it was who drew up the sunblinds and let in the pure air, for which the room thirsted. There was a view over the red roofs right out to sea.

Norman expressed himself delighted. He settled the terms, and paid in advance for a month. He arranged to have meals with the family; he did not want to be lonely, and wanted to learn Alsandrian. All this obviously pleased the old lady, and Norman, too tired even to walk about in the city, shut himself up and slept, to the disgust of Peronella, till the late afternoon.

His bag awaited him at the station a mile away, down on the plain on the land side of the rock. He walked there to get it, still too sleepy to look round him and enjoy the newness of things, and carried it painfully back. He tried that evening to clothe himself as fashionably as he could. He succeeded, at all events, in a country where the proper use of the starched linen collar and its concomitant tie is practically unknown, in impressing the Vidvino Prasko, who in her turn took great care to let him know that she was of old family and good education, and had been Maid of Honour to the last Queen of the country. And so she rambled on, giving Norman, who was eager to hear about the country, an account even of its history and commerce, and left him greatly surprised at the extent of her knowledge. She had been brought up in the Palace itself, in the good old times, as she said, sighing, and knew more than most. For herself, she had a little pension from the Government. "It is worth no one's while to steal it," she observed, "and, besides, I have my daughter, whom I bring up most care-fully—don't I, Peronella?"

Peronella, who had discarded her white frock and now appeared in what had better only be described as her "Sunday Best," blushed modestly and hung her head beautifully. Norman, however, was not pleased, but rather disappointed to find she was not the peasant girl he had thought her, but a half-educated young lady with ideas. Troubled, he looked at her again. She was still there, still beautiful, still charming; but, alas! how the spell of the morning was broken! The nymph who stood before him, the very spirit of Nature, some few hours ago had had lessons in geography and fancy needlework, could even play the piano. She had almost the same accomplishments as those he and all Blaindon had admired in the pretty daughter of Mr Apple.

And yet she was there opposite him, still beautiful, still charming....

Soon after dinner the old lady declared herself sleepy and departed, admonishing Peronella not to stay up too late.

"That's just like mother," said the girl.

"What?"

"She's taken a fancy to you all at once and goes off, leaving me alone with you as if you were a pet lamb instead of a...."

"Lascivious lion," suggested Norman. "By the way, Peronella...."

"Yes."

"Peronella, have you any more lovers?"

"How fond you are of repeating my name! Of course I have. Do I look as if I hadn't? He is called Cesano. He will be coming soon. He will certainly try to kill you. Do you mind?"

"What?"

"Being killed."

"Of course, I should hate it."

"You silly fellow. I mean, you aren't afraid?"

"I am deadly afraid of being killed, so soon after meeting you."

"Would you kill somebody for me if I asked you to?"

"Yes, unless I was likely to be hanged for it."

"I don't believe you're at all brave, or very fond of me, after all."

"I am rather frightened of you, Peronella, at all events."

Some time after, a ring at the bell interrupted some similar inane, mock-passionate conversation.

"You were talking about my lovers, dear Normano," said the girl. "If you want to see one, you have only to wait here while I open the door. Now, if that's Cesano, as I suppose it is, there will be fireworks. Be careful, Normano; he's a rival. Alsandrian lovers are not like English. They have hot blood in their veins. Listen, how he rings. He is angry already. Oh, Normano, go into your bedroom. It would be dangerous for you to stay here—"

"Nonsense; I have come to stay. Do you think I am frightened? I am longing to see this very passionate man and to learn how I ought to make love."

She undid the door and Cesano entered. He was a dark individual, a few years older than Norman, with a bulging forehead, and a black moustache. He looked very much like an English maidservant's idea of a typical Spaniard, being, furthermore, dressed in one of those horrible colour-combinations in velvet and silk that we English, perhaps the best-dressed people in the world, find so charmingly picturesque and so essentially artistic.

"Good evening, Cesano; let me introduce you to our new lodger, an Englishman."

The two men bowed to each other without saying a word. Cesano wasted no time.

"Are you coming out?" he said.

"I should like to, Cesano, but I can't possibly leave a stranger quite alone for his first night in Alsander, can I?"

"Oh, he looks as if he could look after himself, that great pink-faced lout of an Englishman. Besides, what does he matter? And he must be tired if he has only just arrived."

"I am not at all tired," said Norman. "I have been asleep all day."

Cesano gasped. It had never crossed his mind that a foreigner could understand a word of the language of Alsander.

"Then you understand me, sir? Then you don't mind?"

"I do rather. Especially since you have said I didn't matter. Particularly so since you called me a pink-faced lout of an Englishman."

"Forgive me, sir," said Cesano, with intensive courtesy. "I could not have imagined that you understood my words. It is so rarely that we Alsandrians have the pleasure of hearing foreigners speak our tongue. And as you have understood me, you have understood that I was only in jest. And if there was a little offence, you must pardon me. I am a lover. We lovers are so hasty. It is natural to be jealous of all men when one is a lover. Of course, for me to have been jealous of you, even for an instant, was purely ridiculous."

"I pardon you certainly, Signor Cesano," said Norman. "I pardon you with all my heart, but...."

Norman felt uncomfortable. He heartily wished that Peronella would go for her passion-walk with Cesano, and leave him to his too long neglected pipe. But, despite all his Englishman's vague terror of the foreigner, he had all a brave man's objections to hauling down his colours, especially in the face of so ridiculous an opponent as the Italian opera personage who stood there gesticulating at him, and whose politeness was thrice as offensive as his rudeness. So he dwelt a second on the word "but" and glanced at Peronella, who came to his aid only too gladly, and with consummate impudence took up the tale.

"Normano desires to say"—murmured the young lady in a very sweet voice—"that you have plenty of cause for jealousy."

"Cause for jealousy! What do you mean by cause for jealousy? Of him?"

"Ah! he still finds the language a little difficult to speak, you know. Even you who are native do not seem to have mastered it completely, Cesano. Yes, of course, of him!"

"But what do you mean—what do you mean? What do you dare to mean?" cried Cesano, crescendo.

"This!" Here Peronella looked up at Norman with a glance of admiration and put her arm round his waist. Proud of her new lover, she thought also that it would be more prudent to display her colours at once. Cesano staggered to the wall, doubtless moved by real emotion, but with such theatrical gestures that he appeared a mere buffoon.

"What has happened? Can I believe my eyes? Am I moon-mad? Have all the devils possessed me? Are you Peronella? Am I Cesano? Is he your lover?"

He buried his face in his hands. Peronella would not answer the poor fellow.

"What has happened? Has that pink foreigner bewitched your heart? Are you tormenting me or are you tired of me?" he cried.

"Not tired of you," said the girl, growing a little white but not relaxing her grip of Norman, "but very fond of him."

"Fond of that person? Who or what is he? I have not the honour...."

"He is an English lord who came here this afternoon to live here."

"An English lord in this mud-house?"

"It is good enough for him where I am."

Meanwhile Norman was feeling awkward enough. The girl, it seemed, had taken possession of him almost without asking him, though doubtless it was his own fault, for kissing lonely nymphs all in the morning of the world. There she was publicly avowing him, and making him feel very mean and foolish before her honest, if extravagant, lover, who now went on with a sort of portentous dignity:

"I am sorry. Forgive me, Peronella. I am confused. I cannot understand what has happened. You cannot give me up after all these months for some one you do not know at all. It is absurd. It could not be. It is fantastic. It is unreal."

"I did not know I had ever taken you," replied Peronella. "What have we ever done but go out for walks like friends?"

"But I was going to give up everything for you. Do not blast my youth."

"It has been blasted before, Cesano."

"Not like this time. I cannot sleep. Come, take away your arm, last of creatures. I cannot bear it. I will go mad. I will beat you. As for you, sir" (to Norman, in a deep bass), "I will deal with you after with cold steel!"

"Come, now," said Peronella, smoothly. "I am very sorry indeed. One cannot help the hand of Fate."

"Hand of Fate," said Cesano, in justifiable wrath. "It has driven many women to hell, that hand of Fate. Do you kiss a new man every week? Have you a price? Was I not honourable? Did we not talk of marriage? Did I not pick you coral from the sea—violets from the meadows?"

"Don't be poetic, Cesano, or I shall cry."

"Cry! Can you shed tears? I have shed many for you at night beneath your window. But you have no heart!"

"Why trouble then about so stony a young girl?"

The affected languor of her tone irritated Norman almost as much as it was intended to irritate Cesano, but he could not well desert her now, and stood his ground. Cesano sobbed, put one hand on his breast and the other on a tableknife with which he made the most threatening gestures at Norman. The latter, who understood the hand-play more than the rhetoric, could not help laughing at the grotesque but unfortunate Alsandrian.

"Ah! you laugh now!" said Cesano, ferociously. "Some day I will make you smile at the back of your head."

And turning on his heel, to Norman's surprise, he went softly and quietly out of the room.

"I am so sorry for Cesano," said Norman. "I did not mean to be rude to him; he is a good man. I am sorry you were so cruel to him. He has not deserved it of you."

"Love is cruel! And, O, Normano, Love is divine!"

"Love is a very good subject of conversation," said Norman, ungallantly. He was tired, and therefore had sagacious misgivings as to what he had let himself in for. "Good night," he added, and turned on his heel.

"Is that all?" said Peronella, opening out her arms.

But the wary Englishman had fled.

CHAPTER IV

INTRODUCING A GOOD BEGGAR AND A BAD KING

Beautiful and broken fountains, keep you still your
Sultan's dream?
The Golden Journey to Samarkand.

Despite any irritation he might feel in finding his pretty flirtation degenerate into a sentimental romance which might end ill, for a week Norman led the golden life, and, after all, the golden life can only be led in sunny lands, by him who has a mistress on his arm and music in his soul, and it never lasts more than one week in the same place. The golden life in Alsander means swimming, sunstruck memories of old walls and young faces; it means prospects down tortuous streets of blue mountains towering to the sky or of blue skies falling into bluer seas. It means the discovery of an elegant fountain down this way, of a Roman inscription hidden in moss down that. It means the first view of the Cathedral square. For the façade of the Cathedral of Alsander, first seen of a sudden some early morning, when the square is still, seems an impossible thing—a mirage: it is so vast, so lovely, and so old.

But for Norman in Alsander, as for many another, the chill Sunday of disappointment followed the weekdays of delight. Naturally the first disappointment was Peronella. We have already hinted at Norman's disappointment. It did not vanish, that disappointment: it grew. Can beauty be boring? Ah! ye gods, it can, if one has to talk to it, and it is stupid. But was Peronella not romantic? Oh, yes, she was indeed, but romantic with a "k." She was romantick like the fair misses of a hundred years ago. But is not the romantick the same as the romantic in principle? Oh, yes, indeed, the sentiment is the same; but to be romantic requires intellect, and to be romantick requires none. But was not Peronella educated? Indeed she was, most abominably educated, quite enough to ruin all the fresh roses of her nature. She had not, could not, alas! read Ella Wheeler Wilcox, her poems, but, oh! how she would have loved them had she known them! Marie Corelli she did read; you may buy her works in Alsandrian. But was she incapable of appreciating true literature? Oh, no, she adored Shakespeare and Byron, which she read in translations. You see, her mother had ideas and considered herself a lady. Nevertheless Peronella began to bore Norman: the spell was broken!

And once that spell broken, other enchantments lost their hold. The mirage lifted from the city of Alsander. The illusion began to disappear one day when it rained, and the next day, when Norman walked out alone after a sulky quarrel, it had utterly vanished. The rain had ceased, but the sun had revived the smells of Alsander (which were ubiquitous, insinuating, sometimes crushing) without drying the streets. Norman slipped at every step he took in the glutinous mud. The utter disrepair of the cobbled streets made walking bad enough at any time, heartrending after rain. As for driving, it was a wonder there was a carriage in the place. Across one of the narrowest but most frequented roads gaped a fabulously large hole which had perhaps been opened for some vague drainage or burial operations. The displaced cobbles formed a little circular hill all round this preposterous cavity, which looked in consequence more like the crater of Etna than an honest hole in the road, and carriages had positively to be lifted over the hill into the valley and then over the hill again. A couple of men could have put it straight in half an hour—but this was Alsander.

The question will arise, "But what of the pavements?" In Alsander, as a rule, there are no pavements, the roads being flanked on each side by little running sewers. Where pavements do exist they are used for idle shopmen to obstruct with their chairs or pushing shopmen to bar with their merchandise. They also have a way of coming to an end in the gutter after a few yards, just as you are getting your stride in, and then tempting the foolish to wade across the road by casually sprouting up on the opposite side.

Norman had all an Englishman's hatred of discomfort and waste; he felt that Blaindon could put Alsander to shame in the matter of public works; he feared the smells would give him typhoid, and he began to hate Alsander, and he heard the call of Roon, the God of Going, as it is written in the Gods of Pegana.

Besides all this he was frightened and puzzled. He had fallen into a trap. He was looked upon as a prospective son-in-law by the Widow Prasko—and that was ever so largely his own fault. Englishmen were accounted fabulously rich, and this one was evidently handsome as well. Peronella was already airing her proprietorship to the envy and admiration of the other maids of Alsander. Then Cesano was a nuisance with his little tricks, for he was as sincere as he was ridiculous—the complement of Peronella with no redeeming beauty. He was only at the scowling stage at present, but would certainly advance, in accordance with the sound early Renaissance tradition of the country, to powder in the coffee, snake in the boot, or knife in the back. But for all this, Norman was chivalrous and conscientious enough, and no coward, either; and though he felt it would be best for all concerned for him to leave his baggage and run away by the next train, his sense of honour was in conflict with anything that smacked of dishonesty or funk. Besides, he had not so much money left; he had to decide whether he would try and make a living here or elsewhere, and decide soon. It was part of his travel scheme (which was not so fantastic, after all) to work his passage, so to speak, in some way or other from place to place. But as yet he had not earned a farthing or so much as looked for work. This also depressed him.

Thus it was that the great glass dome of his happiness was shattered, and the last hour of the golden life fell like a golden leaf from the tree of existence. And as for that moment when he heard all the bells of morning ringing in his ears and smiled at a girl with her pails of water, that was not a week but five thousand years ago, when all the skies were blue.

Darkly brooding and much disillusioned, therefore, our hero came to the Royal Castle of Alsander. He had not seen it close at hand before. It stands far from the centre of the town, on the steepest part of the rock, an unconquerable edifice of faceted stone, its Palladian gateway flanked by two stupendous fat uncompromising towers, with hundreds of yards of unbroken, unwindowed wall slanting outwards to the base, continuing beyond the towers to right and left. Two sleepy sentries, in a fine old uniform, holding in their hands some weapon, vaguely mediaeval, guarded the entrance.

The strength, one might almost say the ugliness, of the castle pleased Norman's mood. He was just beginning to enjoy the scene, leaning by a fine old statue which stood in the midst of the square on a low pedestal and represented, standing twice life-size, helmeted and hand to sword, the hero King of Alsander, Kradenda the First, the builder of the castle. He was gazing round intently, when an old crouching beggar interrupted him and asked him in a sort of hoarse whisper if he wanted to see the castle. Norman, with a disgusted and pitying glance at the filthy rags of the mendicant, offered him silver to be left in peace.

"I do not want silver," said the old man. "Look you here"—and he tossed into the air a heavy purse that hung by his girdle—"I want to show you the castle."

"Is it open to all visitors?" inquired Norman.

"No, but if I take you we shall pass," replied the vagrant, with assurance. Norman was surprised into accepting; more surprised still when the heavy-eyed sentries gave a sort of furtive salute to his disreputable guide; and most surprised on viewing the interior of the castle. "At all events there was one more thing to see in Alsander before I left," said he to himself.

For inside the frowning battlemented walls, instead of harsh keeps and dungeons, were the beautiful ruins of a beautiful garden. There was a riot of greenery, to which roses, orange blossom, jasmine and hybiscus gave the prominent colours and scents. The grass was sprinkled with cyclamen, asphodel, red anemones and with wild remnants of old cultivation. There were toy stone Greek temples, little cottages like English cottages, painted lath and plaster summer-houses like Turkish summer-houses, showing the bare bones of their construction at every windy corner.

"Who made all this?" inquired Norman.

The old beggar turned away from the garden and pointed to the vast encircling quadrilateral of the wall, as grand from within as from without.

"This wall," he said, standing up straight and waving his hand around with curious enthusiasm, and speaking in a vibrating but refined voice which ill befitted his rags and mouldering beard, "is the work of Kradenda the Great, founder of the power and glory of Alsander, against whose statue you were leaning in the square. Now I know many stories of the great Kradenda, and will tell you one, my lord. In those days the Saracen galleys had driven the people of this land up into the hills, and the plain was all a waste. Now Kradenda was a shepherd lad, and one day he went out at the head of his fellows and burnt the fleet of the infidels...."

"Oh, I have heard the story," said Norman. "Milord is impatient," said the beggar. "But I am glad that after so short a stay in Alsander he should know at least one story of Kradenda the Great. There are, of course, many other stories. My lord, have you heard how King Kradenda recultivated the plain?"

"No, I have not heard that story. Tell me.

"Well, I will tell you. It was like this. Malaria had gripped those good rich lands, and not a soul would reclaim them for fear of disease. The Great King ordered his people to recultivate the plain. But so many died of fever that they murmured against the order. Thereupon he called to them and told them that they were soldiers and would they run from an enemy? 'Never,' they said, 'if he led them,' 'Do you not see, then,' said the King, 'that fever is our enemy now that I have driven off the infidel: you must fight it and die for your country if needs be.' 'We will! obey,' said the old chief who had led the deputation, 'but only if you lead us.' Whereupon? the King laughed and bade them follow him, and there and then he pitched his tent in the filthiest part of the marsh and began to dig a channel for the waters with his own hands. In that way the marsh was soon drained and dry, and such a man was the first Kradenda."

"That is a good story," said Norman, "and well and concisely told. But tell me now about the garden and the summer-houses and the fountain."

"What of them?" said the guide. "The summer-houses are crumbling, the garden is a wilderness and the fountains play no more."

"Weird talk from a beggar," thought Norman. "But who built them?" he inquired aloud. "They are quite beautiful."

"They were built by King Basilandron: he was quite beautiful, too."

"I have never heard of him, though my landlady, who is a wise woman, has told me much of the history of your charming country."

"Ah, we do not talk much of him in Alsander. Here is his name, cut in the wood."

He showed Norman an inscription on the side of a little summer-house with wooden tracery and a faded blue paint, which ran: ΒΑΣΙΛΑΝΔΡΩΝ.

"But why is it in Greek letters?" inquired Norman.

"He would have everything in Greek. He it was who called the river Ianthe. It was known as Vorka before."

"You know the history of Alsander well," said Norman, more and more astonished at the language and erudition of his guide.

"I love Alsander," said the old man. "I know all the stones of this castle and all the stories of Alsander's past."

"Then tell me the story of King Basilandron," said Norman, "for I have never heard it. And after that I shall ask you to tell me the story of your life: for rags do not make you a beggar."

"Neither does my erudition prove me to be a prince in disguise," said the old fellow with a smile. "But I would rather even tell you the story of my life, tragic as it is, than tell you the story of King Basilandron, which is the tragedy of a nation, and one that those who love Alsander do not care to tell."

"Tell me first the story of Basilandron and then the story of your life."

"It is little we poor citizens of Alsander can refuse to the inquiring tourist," said the old man with acerbity. "And may the devil torment you for a member of a great nation that can look after itself. We, you know, are supposed to be incapable of self-government, especially since we went bankrupt a year or two ago, and actually dared to ruin some French bondholders. Since that day the Great Powers have been terrifying us with an international commission. If ever there is a free fight in a café here, or a dog-fight in the square, some foreigner writes to a European newspaper about the anarchy in Alsander. American missionaries, who believe in Noah's Ark and the historical existence of Methusalem, revile the degraded superstitions of our peasants who still hold to their immemorial festivals in honour of the water that bursts from the rock or the grape that grows dark on the vine. And now we are threatened with inspectors, all of varying nationalities, to avoid all appearance of intrigue or possibility of jealousy. You see our strategic importance is the only importance left to us—otherwise we should long ago have disappeared. So we are to have a Spanish Financial Inspector and a Swiss Sanitary Board. Our gendarmerie will be organized by a virtuous Dane. Our agriculture will be modernized by an energetic Dutchman. Our public conveniences will doubtless be improved by one of your own compatriots."

"My compatriot," said Norman, "will not be unoccupied. But I insist upon your telling me the tale of King Basilandron."

"I will tell you, milord, since you are so importunate, but forgive me if I have been impolite. These things touch me so near.

"Well, then, King Basilandron ruled in days when certain ideas from Italy, having reached Alsander, had turned the heads even of sober people and made great havoc of the Court. It was in those days that all this wood and plaster work which you so much admire was erected; it was in this garden that night after night King Basilandron held revel, to the great pleasure of those engaged therein. The Court was all crammed with fiddlers, painters, poets, dancers, barbers and buffoons. But they were quack fiddlers, feeble painters, vile poets and clumsy dancers, who would not have dared to move a leg in Italy. But the barbers and buffoons were such as the world has never seen, so dexterous and stylish. Need I tell you how the country was taxed to maintain this alien population, or how the people groaned and murmured, or how the aesthetic monarch kept them quiet and amused by diverting pageants? All sorts of pageants there were—of beggars, thieves, madmen, lovers, heretics (real heretics, subsequently burnt), queens of antiquity, widows, tigers and Turks. But a pageant was the end of the whole business, as I will tell you now.

"One day the King resolved to re-establish the worship called of Orpheus, to the great joy of his friends. He clothed himself as Bacchus, though per Bacco he looked more like Silenus (if the painters of his day did not make him more ugly than he was, which in those days was not the custom of Court painters). His escort was a troop of noble ladies clothed in forest branches and none too leafy: and one summer evening under the full moon off they went singing to the mountains. After they had danced their fill and sinned God knows what sins, the moon set and back they swooped on the city in a sort of make-believe battle line; and there at the gates was the army of Alsander mumming in Greek tunics waiting to receive their amorous attack. But at that very hour a different host was approaching Alsander—forgotten barbarians from Ulmreich—and the two hosts met. And that is all—and that has been all for the glory and power of Alsander," concluded the old man, bitterly.

"But Alsander is independent still."

"An independence handed her as a gift by Ulmreich and Gantha, her two great neighbours, is not much worth having. The day one of them is strong enough to seize us from the other, we shall go. Or if that international commission really sits, it is as good as death to our little nation. We shall never more be able to raise our heads—and chiefly through the fault of King Basilandron."

"But much might be done now," objected Norman, with a certain breeziness. "Why should Alsander have to wait for an international commission before getting her streets paved? Look at my boots."

"I would rather look at your eyes than at your feet, young Englishman. As for Alsander, she cannot be clean while she is corrupt. That would be hypocrisy, and we have never sunk so low as that. But in Bermondsey the streets are excellently paved. And, by God! Alsander, in all its poverty and decay, is not so vile a place as Bermondsey, nor are its people so brutal or so blind as yours."

"We have no sun," said Norman. "But come, you have been in England, you are a wonderful old man. Tell me your story now that you have told the story of Basilandron."

"I cannot tell my story," said the old man, shaking as if with sorrow. "My tragedy is so little when I think of the tragedy of my people that I can only say—Alas for Alsander!"

"You, sir, are a great patriot," said Norman, touched into respect of all this passion in all those rags.

"I, sir, am a very old man," replied the beggar, and Norman could not tell why the reply was so appropriate.

"I understand now," said Norman, "why you hate these pretty pavilions and love those old walls. And I suppose the present state of Alsander must distress you. But surely some young and vigorous ruler could still do wonders for Alsander? I have been told, to my great surprise, that the King, though young, is insane. I have heard also that he usually lives in this castle, but that the Jewish doctor who attends him, and who is said to be the cleverest man in Alsander (and some say the wickedest), has sent him to England or Ulmreich or somewhere as a last hope. If only a new and vigorous King could rule this land awhile, there is still a chance of greatness; but it is astonishing that the people seem neither to know nor care exactly who or where their King is, or what his true state of health may be. Perhaps you are better informed? I heard myself that the King had been sent to some European asylum to be cured, but no one seems to know to which one."

"As to that point, I can only assure you, my lord, that there is no hope for the King's sanity. It is pure degeneration of race."

"Then I inquired why the heir to the throne was not installed in his place. No one seemed to like to talk of that subject. But it appears she is a girl living somewhere in Ulmreich, very young, and as mad as the King."

"I do not think the young lady in question, whom I once had the honour of meeting, is exactly mad," said the beggar. "A little wild, one might say, and her guardians are wise enough to let her do as she pleases. I expect our illustrious Regent has been spreading that fable."

"You mean Duke Vorza? I understand he is virtually despot of Alsander now. I have heard a great deal of grumbling against him, but nothing very definite, though I have heard some people say that the King is not really so mad as his physician and the Regent pretend."

"Duke Vorza," said the beggar, "is a man of great talent and ambition. He does not like the people of Alsander to talk very much about anything. To have seen him kiss the peasant children in the streets on the day he raised the tax on matches was what you might call a lesson in political economy. It is marvellous, too, how he manages the city council—a rather enlightened body of merchants and professional men and opposed to his reactionary policy. He distributes invitations to dinner at exactly the right moment, and if a dinner fails he decorates. Sforelli (who is only considered a scoundrel because of his dark features and undoubted ability) is almost the only one of them man enough to withstand a title or a decoration. The consequence is he dare not venture out of his house after dark for fear of meeting one of Vorza's ruffians in the street. Oh, there are many dark stories to tell of Vorza, but such is the stupidity of popular rumour it has seized on the most improbable, Vorza and Sforelli, though outwardly amiable to each other, are in secret bitter enemies, and as for the madness of the King, I assure you he is as mad as anyone could pretend him to be."

"But no one seems to have seen him for years," objected Norman.

"I have, but few others," said the mendicant.

"There's something terrible about a King whom his people seem never to have seen," said Norman.

"Listen to me," said the old man in a low and dramatic whisper. "I may not be quite what I seem, as you surmise, and I may have powers even you do not suspect. Would you like to see the King of Alsander and discover for yourself how terrible he is?"

"Do you mean to say he is here?" exclaimed Norman. "Is it not true that he is in Europe—and do the people really not know where he is?"

"Did you not hear that he was expected back?"

"There was a queer rumour, now I come to think of it," said Norman, thinking of his talks with Pedro the cobbler and others, "that he was coming back cured."

"Well, he has returned, not cured, and that is all," said the old man.

Norman started a little.

"I seem to recognize your voice," he said. "Surely I have met you before?"

"Don't you remember, my lord, the old tramp you met in Gantha, who told you all about the beauties of Alsander?"

"Why, that eloquent old fellow, was it you? It was you, then, persuaded me to come to this country. I have much to thank you for: it is a wonderful country indeed. But it was dark on the road that night and I could hardly see you. So you are he. But you were not talking Alsandrian but English."

"I have wandered, and you have learnt Alsandrian."

"Yes. I found the little book you left in my pocket. But tell me, who are you? Of course, I cannot believe you to be a beggar. Enough of these mysterious tricks. You are a man of eloquence and learning. You must be a person of diplomatic importance, if you can really show me the mad King of Alsander."

"You shall really see him as I promised," said the old man, and making a trumpet of his hands he called out "Yohann! Yohann!" in a remarkably sonorous voice. Immediately there appeared from the lodge beneath the gate a sentry at whose girdle dangled two large keys. He came up to them and saluted, but made no remark, and in silence they all three went across the gardens to the vast loopholed wall opposite the gate. The sentry opened an insignificant little door half hidden in the wallflowers that dangled from the crevices between the mighty stones.

"The walls are thicker than you supposed, are they not, my lord?" said the tattered guide.

Norman gasped with astonishment. A huge corridor pierced the wall from side to side and top to bottom,—a corridor at least a hundred feet long and eighty feet high, yet only of a breadth for three men to walk side by side and lit only by a tiny window at the extreme end. Norman having walked over to it saw that the window commanded a sweeping view of the plain of Alsander, the river Ianthe, the sea, the mountains, and also noted that no one could look in through that window whoever might look out, for the wall on that side is built on the top of a sheer precipice of rock. Meanwhile the second key was being applied to another small door half-way down the corridor on the left. It opened groaning; the centre of the corridor was flooded with a shaft of light.

"Enter, my lord," said the mysterious guide. "This is the throne-room."

It was a most presentable type of disjointed majesty, this throne-room, the apotheosis of the ruined summer-house outside, a wreck of what had once been a gorgeous but not entirely tasteless mass of plaster gilding and paint in the style of the late Renaissance. Sham large windows had been let in to hide the little grills in the wall; in the intervening space the two hooks were still visible where once lamps had swung to flood the hall from without with artificial daylight. The ceiling, a false one, for the room went up of old to the height of the wall, like the corridor outside it, was painted with a device in cunning perspective, representing the apotheosis (among very pink angels) of King Basilandron, the same who christened the river Ianthe and was responsible for the disaster of the Bacchic revels. The picture, and indeed the entire room, dated from his lifetime. The wall decorations, however (according to information which Norman subsequently gathered), were added by his son—very tasteful designs of apes and Chinamen—singeries and chinoiseries. Basilandron II evidently disagreed with his father's idealistic tendencies, and held a firm belief that art should not aim at expressing any meaning, not even a lascivious one, but should rather consist of graceful and intricate designs. In this way he anticipated many of the most brilliant modern theorists. Although these panels had suffered considerably owing to the inferior quality of the paint employed, their condition was good compared with the dado, the composition columns, the settees and other accessories of the room. Dust, black, deep and ancient, had settled among those gilded lilies and plaster cupids; part of the work had fallen away, exposing the supporting wires, and part was grievously cracked. It may be because plaster cracks more irregularly than marble, but whatever the reason a noseless plaster Muse, however elegant originally, cannot reassert her loveliness like an antique torso or the armless Aphrodite.

Moreover, the spider, ubiquitous and remorseless, had woven his octagonal mesh in every crevice of the wall, and, more shamelessly still, among the pendants of the great glass chandelier, wherein were still sticking grisly and darkened stumps of candle, the same that had been lit at the requiem of the last King of Alsander twenty years ago. Since then a plain lamp (so portable and so much easier to light) had been deemed sufficient for the service of the Court.

Perhaps the most pitiable objects in the room were the two or three sofas that still remained, their gilt tarnished, their tapestries y mouldy and eaten by the moth. But the hall contained another seat of a far different aspect, impervious to such decay. Beneath the great rose window it stood, at the upper end of the room, strangely out of place, a cold and massive work, the ancient throne of the Kradendas. It was fronted by wide steps, flanked by grotesque yet grand lions, and wrought of granite rock. And if this rude and barbaric throne was anomalous in so artistic a room, still more vivid was the contrast between the majesty of its structure and the majesty of him who sat thereon.

For there sat the imbecile Andrea, with watery grey eyes, with hair and hands unkempt, arrayed in the stifling drapery of his state robes. He was a young man, but he seemed to have been alive five hundred years. His features parodied the portraits of his ancestors. With the heavy iron crown of Alsander on his head, and a great silver sceptre in his hands, he sat immobile; only his mumbling lips seemed to address a phantom and imaginary Court.

CHAPTER V

OF THE KNIGHTING OF NORMAN PRICE

Do diddle di do,
Poor Jim Jay
Got stuck fast
In yesterday.
Peacock Pie.

The madman on the throne seemed to know Norman's guide, for he showed no surprise, but asked immediately:

"Whom hast thou with thee, O last courtier of the Court of the Kradendas?"

"A young squire, O my liege the King, who will devote his life to rescue the house of the Kradenda from infamy and harm," said the beggar.

"He is young, but our need is great. Above all, we need brave men. We need such men as have made Alsander what it is. Tell me," he continued, turning to Norman, "are you brave or fearful?"

"You should humour him," whispered the old man to Norman, who, astonished at the whole scene, and especially at this antiquated and abrupt form of address, did not know what to reply. "He is in the middle ages. For him this hall is still hung with cloth of gold, but he knows that his courtiers have left him, and fears treachery—and, above all, magic. He is a brave man, my liege the King," added the old man aloud.

"Let him speak for himself, then, and do not whisper so much to him in my presence. Sir stranger, are you afraid of dragons?"

"Of none," said Norman, vaguely wondering if he were telling the truth.

"O well, O very well," said the King. "I have need of the strong and resolute. Too long has my kingdom lain in ashes and ruin; too long have I been pent up in this dismal room, a powerless captive, I, the son of the Kradendas! I tell you there has been foul treachery and foul black magic. But it shall end. I will no longer be the sport of a thing who flaps his wings in my face. But his hour has come. No more scales and fins for me. Listen closely. I will whisper to you the vital secret. I had it in a dream. You have only to hit him in the fifth rib. But, whatever you do, do not let him change his shape. You can catch him this evening. Wait behind the curtain. He comes here always at seven o'clock to play chess with me, squares and squares and squares."

"I will be there in waiting."

"Will you take an oath to be bold in my cause, to fight for me, and to serve me faithfully, and my Queen?"

"I will have every care of your Majesty and of your Majesty's kingdom," said Norman, keeping up the spirit of the thing at a further hint from his companion, despite his disgust.

"I think you are not of this country," observed the King. "Come you from North or South, or from the rising or from the setting?"

"From the North, your Majesty," replied the boy.

"Fair scion of the North, I will swear you have no lies upon your lips. What is your name?"

"Norman, if it please your Majesty."

"And are you Knight?"

"I am but squire, your Majesty."

"Then, my deliverer, since for years no one has cared for my ruined Majesty, save this, my last, my oldest, my only courtier, for my leech I count not; since you alone have proffered your service to a deserted and broken King, I am filled with good intentions towards you and propose to bestow upon you now at this moment the ancient and honourable distinction of knighthood, that you may bear me homage. Once more, will you swear to serve me faithfully?"

"Oh, certainly," said Norman, the more uncomfortable in that there was something rather noble about the King's madness.

"Then kneel," said the King, rising, as he said the words, in all his battered splendour, with the deep seriousness of a young child at play. Solemnly and almost gracefully, with the wooden sword that a wise supervision allowed him, he dubbed Norman Knight, according to the famous custom of chivalry, which even in England is not quite dead.

"Rise, Sir Norman," he cried exultantly. "I have long waited for you, my deliverer and friend, for you and for this hour. I have no doubt of your valour: I have every confidence in your success. And as soon as the Dragon is killed the spell will be broken: as soon as the spell is broken my courtiers will return: as soon as my courtiers return their wives will come with them, and troops of beautiful women will kiss my hand. Every morning I will hunt to the sound of the horn—up the valley, down the valley, after the wild boar. Every evening we will eat his succulent flesh in this my ancestral hall. We will fill this room with pageantry yet, and hold such a feast as this cracked ceiling has not supervised for many a long year. And we will put cushions on this uncomfortable throne, and gild it over so as to have it more in keeping with our state and dignity. On the day you kill the Dragon, Knight of the North, all; the cathedral bells shall ring and the fountains shall run with wine, and the populace will shout and brandish flowers all day and wave lanterns all the night. But, ah...."

The voice dropped from ecstasy to fear and went on in a muddled murmur:

"But kill that Dragon soon, Knight of the North. Go out to him soon, go out this evening, before dusk. I would not pass another night like yesternight, with his eyes staring in through my head. He is a basilisk: his glance is death: go quickly. O go quickly—leave my presence—slay that dreadful beast!"

"We will go and slay him at once," replied the old man. "Come, young Englishman," he added in an aside, "I am willing enough to take the hint. I have no taste for this spectacle."

"Above all," the King cried after them, "bring me his head." As they turned and looked back from the door they saw that the King had again collapsed into his throne, and was again working his lips in silence.

Not till they were out in the garden again did Norman speak.

"What does it all mean? Who are you, and what have you shown me?" asked the lad. "This morning the world was as ordinary as a sixpenny magazine: and now my head is turning, and I am walking not like a man in a dream, but, what is worse, like a man in a painted picture. Those flowers are fatal and those walls fantastic. Quick, tell me, what does it all mean? The sunshine is grimacing."

"You have seen," said the stranger, "the Secret of the Picturesque. For now we must talk up on a higher plane."

"Damn the higher plane: tell me who you are. But there, do you think I didn't know it all the time? You can be none other but that...."

"Not a word," said his companion, cutting him dead short. "You did not know it till now, when I intended to let you know. By 'it' I mean either the Secret of the Picturesque or what you meant by 'it.' Besides, it's not true that I am this or am that; that depends on what I am."

"Puzzle me no longer: talk plain sense," implored Norman.

"Surely my words are plain enough. What is it you want to know?"

"Your name and history."

"I have no name, but my friends are allowed to call me the Old Man. My history is a dead secret. But if you are in earnest and willing to talk on the higher plane, I will explain to you the meaning of my remark about the Secret of the Picturesque."

"I am willing," said Norman in desperate bewilderment, and eager to hear any explanation about anything.

His guide seemed as mad as the King and needed humouring no less.

"Come to this bench then," said the Old Poet, "and I will illustrate my meaning with a fable of my own composition."

And taking a manuscript from his pocket, without waiting for a word of acquiescence from Norman, who was getting very hungry, he read as follows:

"There was a man (so majestically made that I knew him at once to be the type of Man) walking along a narrow pathway that led from the valley up towards the hills, following a stream. As he strode along two enchanting girls came flying from the South, poised on dragonfly wings; one of them had a lyre in her hand, which she played merrily, and the other an antique scroll painted over with a multitude of amusing and delicate figures. The man was obviously pleased at the arrival of these spirits; he rejoiced in their companionship (as who would not?), and they all three sang and laughed together on the way. So intent was he on their diverting frolics that while crossing a narrow bridge of planks he nearly fell over into the river, and as time went on, and the pathway began to ascend the hillside more abruptly, I wondered if he was not beginning to find their company a little tedious. For while one of them buffeted him over the eyes with her playful wings, the other flung her robe, for amusement, round his naked body, and embarrassed his movements. However, he got rid of their teasing very soon, and at a point where the path entered a dense forest and they had no room to spread their wings I saw him laugh at their discomfiture. The track grew no better upon leaving the forest, for it was cut in the side of a precipice. The two maidens flew with weary and trembling wings over the horrible gulf, or else tore their dresses and bruised their feet trying to follow over the rocks. The man was hindered by them still, for he had to help them, and to judge by his slow progress and perpetual stumbling he was no skilled mountaineer. I wondered what miracle had preserved him as I watched his perilous ascent; and finally I saw that his right hand was grasping another hand, which had no visible body.

"Very naturally, when they arrived at a little dell very high up in the mountain, where there was a withered tree and a little moss, the girls implored the man to take a little refreshment. But the man's attention was fixed on the last portion of the ascent, a steep snow slope, at the top of which a black rock rose sheer out of the snow; let into the rock was a glittering brass door. So he refused to dawdle, and, gripping the hand, he began climbing at once. The women summoned all their courage and followed on foot: they were too tired to fly any more; and now one, and now the other, was glad of their companion's free left arm. At last they came to the door; the mysterious hand touched a spring; the door flew open to divine music and some one bade the traveller enter.

"But he turned away his eyes resolutely from the superb enchantments of the cave, and swore he would go back unless he could take with him the girls of the dragonfly wings, for the sake and memory of their old and sweet companionship. The poor fairies were bedraggled and muddy, their pretty wings hung limply down their backs; they could hardly smile when the man kissed them.

"'They cannot be admitted without initiation,' said the person to whom the hand belonged, 'and they will not endure.'

"'We will endure any pain, if we may only come in with the Man,' they cried both together, and bent forward trying to pass in and to penetrate the depths of the cavern with longing looks.

"The hand persuaded the traveller to go inside the cave, and promised that his friends should follow. He obeyed, but taking no notice of its beauties stood listening behind the door. He heard the whistling of a scourge and gasps of pain. Then quiet; the door opened, and there appeared his two companions, yet changed, and with a deep fire in their eyes: and they had eagle pinions in the place of dragonfly wings."

"That is very charming indeed," said Norman. "But does it quite explain your remark?"

"If you were to read Plato with attention," said the old man, "you would acquire the habit of seizing the point of a parable."

"I have read the New Testament."

"But this is philosophy."

"And I am sure," said Norman, "that had Plato written that story you have told me, it would have acquired a great reputation. But as for the connexion of the parable and your remark, I conceive that in both you show a dislike of the picturesque, or pretty considering it the foe of beauty."

"The picturesque, my son, is the beautiful but only a section thereof. In this fable I have represented it as miniature beauty. The other fable of the picturesque I have no need to write; it is written over the world from the columns of Baalbek to the arches of Tintern and blazed on every stone of Alsander."

"You mean the picturesque which is decaying beauty?"

"I do," said the old man.

"I understand you, venerable Sir, but why are you so passionate about it all?"

"Don't you see, boy, I love Alsander with a love a little different from the love of the tourist who comes to photograph the ruins. Oh! I have worked for her; but she is dying, dying, dying like a rose on a sapless tree."

"I am afraid you are right," said Norman, sadly. "After what you have shown me I have no hope for unfortunate Alsander."

"Impudent tourist! Do not dare blaspheme against the Queen of cities!" growled the old man. There is more hope radiating from a wayside shrine of Alsander than from all the ten-million heretic barns of your greedy North.

But Norman was used by now to these intermittent bursts of fury. "At all events," he rejoined, "Alsander is no place for an Englishman. I have had enough of it. I have to-day seen its last and most tragic secret. To-morrow I will go."

"You are not going so soon?" There was real dismay in the old man's voice.

"By the first train to-morrow."

"Oh no, no, no! You must stay. I did not mean to speak so soon as this, but I must tell you now. I have great plans for you—a fine work—a whole future. Come: sit on this bench a moment, let me talk to you in earnest. O you cannot possibly be allowed to go at once. Do you not realize the deep seriousness that lies beneath all my mannerisms? Do you think that it was to satisfy a traveller's curiosity that I showed you that poor, miserable madman seated on his throne?"

"I do not know why you showed me the King or why you ever disturbed my life or why you ever do anything you do. But as for work, I prefer to find it for myself. And without wishing to offend you, I want to leave this place. I do not want to be involved in your mysterious schemes." Norman spoke stiffly. The old man alarmed him.

"I will thicken the mysteries round your head like clouds before I permit you to leave Alsander, Norman Price."

"Then it is you," said Norman, startled at the sound of his name. "You are the old fellow who bought the tin of Menodoron off me months ago at Blaindon. You are the tramp who sent me to Alsander. And now you have got me to Alsander you want to drive me to perdition. But I am not going to have my life upset by you any more."

And Norman rose from the bench and confronted the old man with folded arms.

"Indeed, are you not?" was the reply. "Come, I promise you a rare adventure."

"What adventure?"

"I'm not going to spoil the first chapter of the story by looking up the last page. Trust and obey me as you trusted and obeyed me before—the greybeard with the blue eyes. Did my advice turn out so badly? Do you presume to tell me that you are sorry I drove you to Alsander?"

"Oh, as for that, I've had a glorious journey. But the time has come for me to go. I have no money left. And I have personal reasons."

"I know, I know." The old man tapped with his stick. "Some pretty wench, is that the matter? Has it come to this so soon?"

"You have guessed rightly."

"Foolish boy. Is such a game worth your pursuing—you with a mind! Not to mention that it's poor sport hunting doves. There's but one way for such as you with a maid. Try the intellect first—then ask the heart. Love's ways are folded in the mind. Second-rate poets may walk in their gardens prelassing up and down, singing you songs of the scholar that loved a farmer's girl. But you and I are wise enough to know love from lust, Norman Price. Lust has her whims, even her selections—that I grant you: but shall she delude us into taking her for Love?"

"Lust is a great Goddess as well as Love."

"It may be; but she is a great foe of reasonable men. And Love comprises all her power and many other powers besides. But, believe me, your difficulty is not a disaster, and tact can meet it, and I swear you will learn what love means before you leave Alsander."

"Your promises are pretty bold, especially that last one, my Poet. However, if you promise me good sport, of course I will stay a little longer in Alsander."

"I have one bag full of promises and one full of fulfilments," smiled the old man, "and they both weigh pretty well the same. But first you have a promise to make to me."

"Which is?"

"That you will maintain the most absolute, the most impenetrable secrecy concerning what you have seen this afternoon, including the very existence of such persons as myself and the King of Alsander."

"A reasonable and not unexpected request. Of course I give you my word of honour to keep silent. But reveal your next mystery, Signore!"

"What is a revealed mystery, except for the Church? All I care to let you know is that if you prove your mettle you shall be allowed to help in the regeneration of Alsander."

"A political scheme—is that it? But how am I to prove my mettle?"

"Wait and you will see."

"Tell me at least," rejoined Norman, "what is to be my immediate conduct. How am I to make the first step of this sublime journey?"

"Return to your lodging, rise, eat, walk, sleep, and flirt a little less than usual, and await events."

"Is that all?"

"Not quite all. I have another very fanciful request to make. Are you what the ancients call a good hypocrite, that is to say, an accomplished actor? For there is a delicate piece of acting which I would like you to perform. I want you by gradual degrees to raise a little mystery about yourself. I want you to insinuate with a hint here and a whisper there that you are a personage, a man with a past, a nobleman in disguise, at all events not quite what you seem. Let the honest folk you dwell with begin to imagine that there is some secret about your arrival in Alsander."

"My dear sir, what a very odd idea!"

"You will be full of odd ideas in a few weeks' time. I only hope that you will succeed in this the first of your tasks, and that you have not already been too explicit concerning your origin and identity. Play the lost millionaire or the ruined marquis. Become quickly a marked man—a man at whose approach the townsfolk whisper."

"This is a harlequin's game," said Norman, indignantly.

"Well, the world's a ball, and out of shape at that: there's no need to be ashamed of mummery. If you don't like it leave it: but I should be extremely sorry, and you would miss the occasion of your life. Come, now!"

They passed through the castle gate. The sentries appeared to be still asleep, leaning against the archway, their lances propped on their drowsy bodies. The castle square was deserted as ever. Halfway across the old man stopped—seized Norman by the lapel of his coat and observed, "By the way, you ought to give that girl a handsome present!"

"What queer jumps you do make in the conversation, to be sure!" exclaimed Norman. "When your great and secret scheme has enriched me, no doubt I shall make her a very magnificent present. But I can't see the immediate necessity, and at present I am pretty short of cash."

"Never mind the cash. Go to a little shop in a back lane opposite the cathedral and ask to see fine presents for fine ladies. He buys stolen goods, sells cheap, gives unlimited credit to anyone who says 'The Poet sent me.'"

"Why, I have already noticed that little shop," cried Norman. "It contains all sorts of trash, and the other day I found a few old books exposed in the window, and an old Amsterdam Petronius among them."

"Yes. Those pretty old vellum bound classics, I should tell you, must be bought with caution and bought cheap. They have no intrinsic value if you want to sell them again. But he has all sorts of treasures; I can recommend him to you strongly. By the way, it may seem odd of me to ask, but will you excuse me a moment?"

"Certainly," said Norman, and the old man walked swiftly away from him and hurried up a back street. Norman kept wondering why his guide was so insistent on the question of the present. He then wondered why he had gone, and then, as minutes went on, he wondered why he had not returned. He looked up the back street. There was no trace of his strange companion, who evidently did not intend to reappear, and had taken this odd way of vanishing.

"Well," said Norman to himself as he paced home pondering on the fantastic events of the afternoon, "in this fair city of Alsander at least I can pass as sane!"

CHAPTER VI

CONCERNING ISIS AND APHRODITE: WITH A DIGRESSION ON THE SHOCKING TREATMENT THE LATTER'S FOLLOWERS RECEIVE FROM THE HANDS OF ENGLISH NOVELISTS

I had read books you had not read,
Yet I was put to shame
To hear the simple words you said,
And see your eyes aflame.
Forty-two Poems

And there was Peronella!

Seated at the window charmingly dressed in white and rose, with the sun on her face and neck and naked arms, with light playing with those said marvellous arms of hers and making all the little downy hairs on them sparkle. "Beauty is Truth," says the poet, and Norman, looking on her with all the passion of a passionate man, longed to believe the poet's lie and banish the disappointments of the mind. There was nothing vulgar or half-educated about her beauty—lips or hands or eyes. Was she not perhaps simply a child, a soul asleep, repeating like one in an hypnotic trance the rubbish she had been forced to learn? Was she not merely waiting for some violent shock of love or life to dispel the false personality of the genteel young Miss and unveil the true Woman, with all the unconquerable nobility of the peasant and the curious greatness of the South?

Norman sighed as he gazed on the lovely girl and immediately proceeded to eat an ample meal, washed down with ample wine. We have mentioned that he was very hungry. He was thirsty, too, and the white wine of that country is a good wine, if a little sweet. Then he took a book and read and looked at his mistress, exchanging some sufficiently foolish remarks from time to time. But he was worried with the strange events of the fore-noon, impatient to meet his strange mentor again and not knowing where to find him. Too soon also he became troubled by the philosophical question, May Beauty be stupid? and altogether he was not in a mood to be absorbed by any book at all.

Peronella, a few moments later, looking up, saw that his eyes had wandered, that the little book was on the floor, and that his face expressed deep thought. One does not often see people thinking in Alsander, and Peronella wondered if it hurt. Coming to the conclusion that it must be uncomfortable to wear such a face, she got up and went to stand by Norman's chair. Such a domestic scene has many an artist of Holland painted to please the quiet burghers of The Hague. Norman kissed her somewhat mechanically, and without that intense devotion and fiery rapture to which she was accustomed.

"What have you been reading that interests you so much and makes you kiss me in that stupid way?" she cried.

"It is a little Latin book I brought with me from England."

"In Latin? What's it all about? Is it very dull?"

"Sit on my knee and I will tell you all about it. No, don't ruffle my hair, but attend to lessons. I was reading about a great goddess who rose up from the sea, whose robe was so black that it shone...."

"But I thought she was quite naked."

"Who?"

"The goddess who came out of the foam."

"Why, who has been telling about the goddess who rose from the foam?"

"Father Algio in one of his Lent sermons told us a great deal about her."

Father Algio was an old monk with whom Norman had talked once or twice: a gentle soul, but with an odd fire lurking about his eyes. One realized that if roused by the trumpet of the Church he would have marched like a Crusader to uttermost Taprobane, fighting for the Lord.

"What had he to say about the Lady Aphrodite?"

"Aphrodite, yes, that was her name. How clever you are! Oh, the priest said that he thought the reason why we were so given to the sins of the flesh was that we were of the old Greek blood, and had never forgotten the worship of this lady who came from the sea."

"What an intelligent priest it is! O Peronella, you are a true daughter of Aphrodite."

"Tell me about her, Normano. She was the goddess of Love!"

"Yes, and she has a son called Cupid and is drawn in a chariot by violet-throated doves. Also, Peronella, she has a little silver broom, with which she drives away the cobwebs from a man's soul when he has read too many books."

"And when did she wear the shining black?"

"O! this book is not about Aphrodite, it is about Isis, an Egyptian goddess."

"Egyptian? That must be interesting. Was she as beautiful as Aphrodite? Tell me all about her."

"There are different sorts of beauty. Aphrodite was a graceful, careless and happy woman, rather like you to look at, and very much like you in character."

"How charming of you to say so!"

"While Isis had all Nature to manage, and the moon and the sea. She was a terrible goddess, with snakes in her hair, and a great disc between her breasts. Men loved her none the less; she was the spirit of all Nature, and required purity and endurance from her worshippers."

"Purity and endurance! And snakes in her hair! Aphrodite must have been far more pleasant, especially if she was like me. She was the patroness of our city, the Father said; and Dr Sforelli wrote to the papers once to say that the image of the Virgin in the Cathedral Church was a heathen statue that some King put up there and that clothes had been made for it later. I know that because Father Algio was so furious at the time that he preached three sermons against the Jews. But why do you read such rubbish?"

Norman was irritated by the naïveness of the remark, and still more irritated with himself for being irritated.

"What an ass I am," he said to himself, "to talk to a pretty girl about the Classics, and what a much larger ass to trouble what she thinks!"

Norman had to learn that education makes prigs of all of us, whether we will or no. Of wise and learned men only the truly great can keep their characters free of priggishness, and even then, what of Marcus Aurelius and William Wordsworth and John Ruskin? What even of Olympian Goethe?

And there she was, shining, shining.

"You mean," said Norman, "why do I read such rubbish when I have you to look at?"

And still Peronella shone.

"The book of your eyes is the best book," said Norman.

Romance even in her moment could not so fool him that he did not wish he could have said "the book of your soul."

Peronella shone, and, by an instinct, shone in silence.

"You are the prettiest girl I have ever seen," said Norman.

And the sun shone on Peronella.

Then though indeed for a moment more Norman heard the voice of caution, it was but a voice fading far away. Some arguments against caution ran through his mind—pompous self-depreciation and some inverted snobbery about "good enough for a grocer boy." Then the petty arguments were needed no longer: his mind faded and went out, and he leapt upon her like a god from Olympus on some not reluctant spirit of wood or water. He pressed her to him till he felt as if every inch of the fiery contact were complete, and he forgot whole oceans of civilization in a moment. That is what education is made for, some might say, it gives us more to forget and more to abandon in crucial moments of love or heroism.

He kissed her all round her burning face. He kissed the soft skin behind her ear where first he kissed her in the dawn—in the best and earliest hour of all the golden days. He kissed her smooth and naked arms that bound his neck like a silver chain. He set all the snow of her shoulder afire with kisses, and on her mouth he forgot the wise advice of Browning and gave her the bee's kiss first.

The maddening sun still shone on Peronella, on her soft dishevelled robe whence gleamed what a man might take for a red rosebud; on her dark hair with the hyacinthine shadows where a man might see all the stars that shine in a Syrian night—on her cheek and throat and her silver arms—but not on her eyes, for, heavy with passion, they were all but closed.

On Norman, too, shone that great and primitive Ball of Fire—on Norman, as bright an Adonis as ever ran riot in a gallant tale.

But when they paused for breath, as even the bravest lovers must, and sat together on the little blue divan that graced the barren room; when Peronella's lips were free to speak, and Norman's mind was free to meditate—if only for a brief, sharp, cruel moment—how swiftly went the sun behind a cloud!

"When will you marry me?" said Peronella, "and will you take me to England? O, say you will take me to England, Normano, and when you drive me round in your carriage all the world will say, 'That woman cannot be of our town; she is the most beautiful woman that we have ever seen.'"

"Darling," said Norman, "let me think of this moment, of nothing but this moment, and always of this moment," and he kissed her again.

But the sun shone no more on Peronella! And her lover was not thinking only of the moment. He was thinking of his life. Her pretty words pierced him like little darts of ice, and all the comminations of the sages could not have frightened him more than the maiden's innocent speech.

He saw in his clear-sighted panic that here was an end of all bright dreams save this one: and he knew how soon this dream would fade. He saw Peronella unhappy—a Peronella who could not be afforded a carriage—sulking behind the counter of the Bon Marché, in the rain. He saw how her beauty would fade away in England, swiftly, in a few years—and all in a moment she seemed as she sat there to grow old and tired before him, wasting away beneath the low, dark northern skies. He judged her character with Minoan rightness. He knew she would always be a child, always be silly, querulous, unfaithful, passionate: he knew, above all, how soon she would kill that spark in him that made him different from other men—that spark the poet bade him cherish. And he feared she would bore him at breakfast every morning of his life.

Ah! Peronella was good enough—nay, a prize beyond all dreams!—for a Blaindon grocer: he knew that. But all the brilliant fantasies and conquering ambitions which his heart kept so secret that he would not have spoken of them to his old friend (are there not wild miracles which we all, even the sanest of us, hope will happen for our benefit and glory?), all these hidden desires and insane fancies came beating upon the doors of his soul.

Had he been a southerner himself, of course he would have taken the girl and left her at his pleasure, the moment the love-glow faded and the romance grew stale. Her body was his for a kiss, for a smile, at the worst for a traitor promise or a roseleaf he. But he was an Englishman—and perhaps only Englishmen can fully understand why Norman, for all that the thought quivered in his mind, withstood, as we say in our canting phrase, temptation.

For my part, I think the phrases we use, specially in books, are canting enough, and the foreigners rightly scorn us. In no tale since Tom Jones have we had an honest Englishman who makes love because it is jolly and because he doesn't care. With what a pompous gravity and false seriousness do we talk, we

English men of letters, of a little lovemaking which in France they pass with a jest and a smile. Think how our just and righteous novelists fulminate against the miscreants of their own creation. Think of Becky Sharp and her devilish intrigues, of Seaforth and his vile deceitfulness. For Thackeray, the Irregular Unionist (if so we may style those easy livers) is a scourge of high society: for Dickens, he is an ungodly scoundrel, a scourge of low society; for Thomas Hardy, he is a noble fellow disregarding the shackles of convention; while the late George Meredith invariably punishes the amorous by describing them as intellectual failures. To-day Mr Shaw would consider Lovelace disreputable owing to his lack of interest in social problems, while the pale Nietzscheans would worship him with ecstatic gasps as a monstrous fine blonde beast. Our popular novelists are entirely unaware that such horrible scoundrels exist, and our legislators will shortly pass a law which will enable all offenders against monogamy to be flogged. Their agitation will be called a "revival of the old Puritan spirit," and their law will be applied with rigour to the lower classes. The French, I say, call us filthy hypocrites.

And yet the accusation, if levelled against our race and not only against our writers, is not a true one, however plausible. We are more restrained than other races, and that neither because we are less passionate nor because we are more timorous. Our athletic youths are purer—do not merely say they are purer, than the diminutive young men abroad. It is really true there is a special kind of nobility-and generosity in the way our gentlemen treat women. There is something in our race that makes us different from other nations. Call our severe principles a fear of convention, an outworn chivalry, if you like; you have not accounted for all cases; perhaps it is true that an Englishman is more likely than any other European to love a woman deeply enough to be content with her for ever. At all events, it should be remarked how those Englishmen who through education or travel have most tolerance for the sins of others and most opportunity for sinning themselves seldom lose their own traditional scruples. And that is why (to come back to our hero) Norman, who would never have dreamed of blaming Tom Jones for his jolly conduct, and who had read with zeal and appreciation novelists of France who held the most scandalous theories concerning the unimportance of it all, was nevertheless unable to make love to a girl whom he intended to desert. Besides, it struck him, the girl had never yet yielded to a lover. For him the dilemma was clear: he must marry this girl or leave her, and the thought came over him like that

One clear nice
Cool squirt of water o'er the bust,
The right thing to extinguish lust.

Now had he accepted this dilemma bravely, and fled that very hour from the siren presence, he would have had only a flirtation and a few kisses to store up against the hour of remorse. But he fought shy of drastic measures and sought to gain time like a Turkish diplomat. Perhaps, too, he wanted to stay in Alsander yet a little longer to inquire into the mystifications of his tramp guide, and await instructions as to the promised "career of good works." At all events, there is no doubt that as far as the procrastination business went, he found suddenly a great inspiration in the curious parting command which the old poet had given him. He would weave a mystery about himself. He would thus not only obey the fantastic injunction of the poet, but find a most practical means of escape from a perilous position.

He shook himself free of the twining arms, roughly and suddenly, as though he had just remembered something, and paced up and down the room as one lost in thought.

"Why, what is it?" said Peronella. She was always alarmed at seeing a man meditate. Such is the profound instinct of women!

But Norman, intent now on playing his part with thoroughness and efficiency, made no answer, and going over to the window frowned gloomily and began to mutter to himself.

"Tell me what is the matter," cried the girl, running over to him. "Are you ill?"

"Ah!" said Norman. "I wish I could tell you what is the matter. There is more the matter than you know of, dear, and my heart is as heavy as lead."

"Why, what ever has happened?" said the girl, and her face grew longer still.

"Forgive me, Peronella. I should not have spoken."

"You say your heart is heavy as lead. Tell me what is troubling you!"

"Oh! a little secret trouble, that is all."

"What trouble can be secret between you and me?"

"Do not speak of it again, dear. Forget it. I am sorry I hinted that anything was wrong."

"You are not deceiving me, Normano? You do not love an English girl?"

"No, it is not that."

"Then what is it? You must tell me."

Norman sat on the table and put his hands on the girl's shoulders.

"Well, then, who do you suppose I am?" he asked, with a half-smile.

"Why, an Englishman, of course."

"An Englishman. But what Englishman? And why should I come to Alsander and live in Alsander?"

"But why not? Other Englishmen have come to Alsander."

"Yes, but to buy and sell."

This crude artifice was quite enough to trouble the wits of Peronella.

"It is very strange," she said, musing, "and Cesano said it was strange, but who are you, then, by all the Saints?"

"That I cannot tell you, Peronella."

"Well, what have you come for if not to buy and sell? Besides," added Peronella, passionately, "I love you, and that is enough. What do I care who you are?"

"If your love were deep, perhaps you would care who I was."

The saying of this sentence was the worst thing Norman ever did in his life. His conscience haunted him for years and never let him forget those dozen careless words and their cynical hypocrisy.

Peronella did not understand him, nor attempt to, but blazed out in a fury, "How dare you come and tell lies and pretend to be what you aren't and deceive us all? It's all lies, you don't care for me one bit, and I am a little fool!" cried Peronella, on the brink of tears and truth.

"How have I deceived you?" said Norman, lamely.

"You never told me who you were. You come and pretend to be what you are not. You make love to me, and now I see you want to run away."

"You never-asked me. I am not running away," said Norman, breathlessly, seeing this card-house toppling.

"I ask you now."

"Look here," said the hypocrite. "Listen to me and trust me. No, you know I am not lying to you. Look into my eyes and see. I ask just one thing of you. Wait three months and you shall have an answer and know who I am."

"Don't tell more lies and talk more nonsense, species of brute," said the girl, savagely.

"Ah, Peronella, I wish I were talking nonsense."

And the infernal fellow put on an air of sorrow and nobility.

"Wait three months," he repeated, "and then see if you want to marry me, or dare to want to marry me," he added with magniloquence, thoroughly ashamed of himself but too deep in the mire to get free.

"O, Normano, what do you mean? Shall I kill you or believe you?"

"Wait a little while, dear," he said, bending over her with a not feigned tenderness. "Wait a little while and you shall see."

Steps were heard on the stair.

"Here is Cesano," said Peronella, and forthwith Cesano came in with an ineffable air of being on his best behaviour. Norman took his opportunity and went, and with a bow which his fuming rival took for supercilious generosity bade them both good-night.

In the loneliness of his bedroom he fell on his bed like a penitent child and cursed himself for a mean scoundrel. As for Peronella, the first words she said to Cesano were:

"There is a mystery about my Englishman, I wonder who he is," and thereupon she repeated to him the whole conversation. True, he had not told her to keep the secret, but in any case she could not have kept one. It was to be the first thing Cesano was to tell Petro the cobbler when he saw him later that evening, and the first thing Petro the cobbler told Father Algio when he came in for a cup of coffee towards midnight, and the first thing Father Algio told to all his numerous acquaintance. Norman woke up next morning famous and a mystery, and was stared at in the street even more than before. Peronella was perhaps pleased to pass for the mistress of a mystery, Cesano's hopes revived and all seemed for the best in the best of all possible worlds—for three spacious months to come, at least. So thought Norman.

CHAPTER VII

THE SOCIETY FOR THE ADVANCEMENT OF ALSANDER

This impossible story of a mad king and a throne going begging.

An anticipated critic.

The unfortunate indisposition of the old King of Bavaria....

The Prince of Wied is spoken of as a likely candidate for the throne of Albania.

The Daily Papers.

There is a King in a Tragedy of Maeterlinck who woefully exclaims, "Wherever I am, nothing happens." But the old fellow was accustomed to uneventfulness; Norman had reason to expect something better of life, and the mysterious words of the old poet had led him to hope for thrills and sensations. The four days succeeding the day of the interview with Peronella, described in the last chapter, drew blanks in the game of his destiny. On the fifth day he was walking moodily about, trying to extract amusement from the inquisitive glances with which a subtly deceived populace already eyed him, when he heard a voice at his shoulder saying in good English, "Keep it up," but though he turned quickly he could see no one in the street who appeared at all guilty of the observation, which might have been ventriloquial.

Another week passed, and the old resolve to leave Alsander again took possession of Norman's mind. Remorse at his hypocrisy, and longings for Peronella, gnawed his heart: while he felt that if he did not speedily retire from the scene startling harm would come of what was really a loveless passion. He decided, however, not to leave her without getting her a present, which he shrewdly (but I think unjustly) suspected would compensate the girl for the loss of a lover. And of course he remembered that the old Poet, whom by now he had almost given up as a fraud, had given special advice in this matter too. Well, he could but follow it, and see if there was anything to be found for Peronella in the little dark shop the Poet had recommended, and which he himself had discovered almost his first day in Alsander. He therefore invited her to come with him and choose herself a present.

When they arrived in front of the little shop it looked more fascinating than ever. It had evidently been rearranged, and seemed to Norman to exhibit more amusing things in its narrow frontage than all the other shops in Alsander set on end. For it contained snuff-boxes, shawls, dirty old silver, tattered bits of embroidery, carved walking sticks, some worm-eaten books, last century oak settees, Turkish zarfs, Hittite cylinders, Chinese saucers full of Greek and Roman coins, real stones and bits of glass, animals in beaten bronze ware from Damascus, very old leather bottles from England, some forged Egyptian antiquities, some very horrible cameos, some rather pretty intaglios, about three quarters of what had been a fine Persian rug, and boxes of things and cases of things and bales of things and trays of things, and all of them finely powdered with a most pestilential dust.

They entered. Peronella, spitting and sneezing without restraint, exclaimed loudly and bitterly (with utter disregard to the feelings of the shopkeeper, a pretty, slender, dark-eyed, young fellow, who seemed quite out of place among his musty surroundings) that there was nothing to be found there and what he had dragged her there for she couldn't imagine when there was that nice new shop where they sold wonders from Ulmreich ever so much nearer home. Norman, undaunted, was preparing to turn the shop upside down to show Peronella what marvels were to be found there if one only knew, when he was surprised to hear the shopkeeper exclaim quietly and rapidly in English, "Send her away, I want to talk to you." Now this was indeed startling, for it was only an accident that had led him to the shop on that particular day. However, at all events, Norman, eager to fathom the mystery, rose to the occasion. Perhaps this was the poet's hand and he had recommended the shop on purpose.

"Look here, Peronella," he said, immediately. "If you don't like the dust (and it is dusty here) why don't you go home without me? I'll stay here and find something. Besides, I would much rather bring you home a surprise."

"But suppose I don't like it," she objected. "You told me I might choose, and I'm sure there is nothing in this dusty, musty rat cupboard of a place."

"I'll arrange that it can be changed. Or I'll get something you do like as well," he added, with ridiculous vainglory, for his hundred pounds were ebbing faster than the sands of time.

"Very well," said Peronella, half convinced and pouting. "If you don't want me, I'll go." And more in pique than compliance she left him alone with the fine young shopman, who was really a remarkably graceful young man, and one who obviously had no doubts as to his own good looks. Indeed he had ostentatiously set them off by wearing the national costume of Alsander—puffed breeches, pleated silk shirt, and a short loose coat with wing-like sleeves, of dark blue gracefully lined with gold. This costume appeared all the more striking to Norman, as he had never seen one before; for it is rarely worn by the Alsandrians except on ceremonial occasions.

"What service can I be to you, sir?" said Norman. Himself a shopkeeper, he knew the value of a gentlemanly treatment, and did not allow his curiosity to get the better either of his self-control or of his manners.

"The question," replied the dealer in antiques, in a very soft and gentle voice, "is not so much what you can do for me as what you can do for yourself."

"And what can I do for myself?" inquired Norman, wondering at the fine but feminine beauty of the young man.

"The question is not really so much what you can do for yourself as what you can do for Alsander."

"The question is," retorted Norman, with some heat, "exactly how long the pantomime season is going to last?"

"The reply in general is for as long as woman gives birth to child: in particular, for as long as the A.A.A. is uncertain of your devotion."

"And what is the A.A.A.?"

"It is," replied the shopman, "the Association for the Advancement of Alsander."

"I am sure that it is an admirable society."

"Like all earthly institutions," observed the dandified young shopman, with a sententiousness ill befitting his years, "it has its defects, but want of precaution is not one of them."

"And where does it meet?"

"Here," said the shopman, briefly.

"And when does it meet?"

"Now," was the reply, followed almost immediately by a clatter and a crash as if all the machinery of a steam-mill had started with a jerk. Norman had just time to see the shutters going down; then he found himself in total darkness.

"What in Hell do you mean by this?" he cried out, thunderstruck: but the shopman gave no answer or other sign of existence, and Norman suddenly realized with dismay that he was alone and a prisoner. For a moment or two he groped and fumbled in the dark. Then he remembered his matches. He found three and lit them one by one. They cast all sorts of curious and flickering shadows from odd-shaped objects like crocodile gods and water-skins; one by one they went out. Norman was only the wiser in as far as the little light had lasted long enough for him to find out that the end of the shop had no exit and that his interloctuor had certainly disappeared, and he therefore spared himself the trouble of stumbling about in the dark for a means of escape. "This is fun," he thought boyishly, and sat down on what he had seen to be a horribly dusty and cracked Chippendale chair to await proceedings. When ten minutes had passed he began to scratch his head; after twenty minutes the room had grown insufferably stifling and the philosophic mood had passed: after half-an-hour he had formulated a scheme in accordance with which he would use the hindquarters of a large brass elephant, probably Indian, which he had noticed faintly glimmering on a shelf, as a battering ram. His idea was that with so heavy an implement he could break a hole in the shutters, which seemed to have closed automatically, or at least by hammering attract the attention of some passers by in the street outside. He was about to act on this ingenious plan and had already grasped the elephant firmly by one leg when his ear was attracted by a noise of heavy breathing from behind the shop, and a fumbling sound which suggested the turning of keys. The next instant a sort of panel-door opened at the back of the shop, flooding the place with a light that made Norman blink, and a butler, who, with his side whiskers, livery and portly presence looked so like a butler that he positively made Norman gasp, said in the most servile and insinuating English, "Would you step this way, sir?"

Norman stepped, hoping that a chance had come at last of discovering the meaning, if any, of what he now felt sure was a superb and intricate joke. He followed the butler-like butler down a bare corridor and was ushered into a large room, which he judged from a symbol AA, which was hung on a bit of cardboard on the wall opposite and was the first thing that struck his eye, could be nothing else than the head-quarters of the Alsander Advancement Association. But the room, which was neither sumptuous nor sordid, but eminently respectable, was a disappointment to Norman, and so were the presumed Associates, to whom the same adjectives were applicable. They were sitting at the end of the room behind a long table for all the world as if they were a board of examiners, and were all dressed in badly-cut frock coats. In front of each was a sheet of clean foolscap, pen, ink, and blotting paper. The young shopman sat in the centre in a slightly more comfortable chair, radiant in his extravagant costume as a parrot among crows; but Norman scanned their faces in vain to find the old Poet whom he naturally expected would be present on this mysterious occasion.

"Take a chair, my man, take a chair," said a wizened little old fellow, with a fussy, irritable voice.

"Certainly," said Norman, not pleased with the style of address, and he seated himself opposite the shopman, where the single unoccupied chair in the room was placed.

"I hear," observed the little old man gain, but in grave and serious tones, "that you are a candidate for the Crown of Alsander."

CHAPTER VIII

HOW NORMAN FAILED TO PASS A QUALIFYING EXAMINATION FOR THE POST OF KING OF ALSANDER, AND WAS WHIPPED: TOGETHER WITH A DIGRESSION ON THE EXCELLENCE OF WHIPPING

Les cris ne sont pas des chants.

Paul Fort

Norman was about to laugh at this unusual question when he seemed to catch the eyes of the Board of Examiners at once (for he could think of them under no other designation). All the eyes seemed to be looking at him with such peering intentness that he began to believe that they were all unintentional and not intentional lunatics, and therefore dangerous. So he simply bowed. If it is a joke, thought Norman, that will be in keeping; if it is not, it will be expected of me. And he thought himself clever.

"Very good," said the little man, abruptly. "I think, Doctor," he continued, turning to a prominent Hebrew on his left, "that the preliminary examination should be conducted by you in person."

"I will begin at once. Take off your clothes," said the Doctor, addressing the last remark to Norman in a tone of command.

"But really...." began Norman, in expostulation.

"Absolutely necessary, I assure you," continued the Doctor. "For the proper exercise of monarchical functions nothing, not even courtesy, not even common sense, is more important than a sound physical condition. To judge of that condition it is imperative that you should take off your clothes. I may add," he continued, not unkindly, "that considering your general appearance I do not think that you will have much difficulty in satisfying the examiners on that score."

Norman was so puzzled by the evident gravity of the heavy-bearded doctor's speech and demeanour that he began to believe that a certain mad seriousness underlay the whole proceedings. It seemed to him unlikely that a dozen lunatics possessed of a common mania should find such a facility of meeting together in solemn assembly, even in Alsander. The poet, whom he still believed to be the prime instigator of this curious comedy, though eccentric, was no madman. So, having rapidly summed up in his mind the pros and cons of the case, Norman cautiously took off his coat.

However nothing less than complete nudity would satisfy the Doctor, and Norman, with growing reluctance, shed garment upon garment till, in the words of the Eastern poet, "the shining almond came out of his dusky shell," and "the petals of the rose lay strewn? upon the ground." However, at a word from the shopman, who seemed in authority, Norman was permitted to retain as much clothing as would satisfy the by-laws of a very free bathing resort. The Doctor then rose, came round the table, and, seizing hold of the unfortunate, tapped him, pinched him, prodded him, poked him, felt his muscles, sounded his chest, examined his tongue, blew in his ears, slapped his stomach and tried his pulse. All this to the intense aggravation of his victim.

But when the Doctor finally commanded him to rim round the room as he was and climb along the rope that dangled from the ceiling, the boy succumbed to over-mastering indignation.

"I am not going to stand any more damned nonsense from you or anybody else," cried Norman. "This joke has gone quite far enough, and though it may amuse you vastly to make a fool of me I'll knock down the next one of you who tries it on."

The effect of his words was as instantaneous as he could have wished; there could be no mistaking the anger that flashed in the eyes of these curious examiners. Even Norman, in the heat of his excitement, noticed that, though he failed to notice that the youthful President's face (for the young shopkeeper seemed to be President, to judge from his central chair) remained unmoved save for a slight ocular twinkle. It was the President, however, who addressed him: "I am afraid," he said, "that we shall have to ask you to dress and leave us at once."

"I won't leave the room until you apologize to me, and if you don't apologize I'll punch your head." And Norman, all but naked as he was, began to bend up and down a very decent right arm and seemed well capable of executing his threat.

"You should be more patient, sir," observed the President, waving towards Norman his gold-embroidered sleeve with a conciliating smile. "I assure you that it is to your advantage to obey us, and very much to your disadvantage to be rude. I admit that our demands, coming from total strangers, seem both impertinent and extravagant, but I assure you that they are necessary, and I should like to impress you with the earnestness of this apparently inane procedure. The Doctor only desires to see your muscles in motion. I assure you, your body is not a thing of which you need be ashamed. Should you disobey, you will be in serious danger."

"I don't believe you. You dare not touch me. I am an Englishman," retorted Norman, refusing to be conciliated.

"I am afraid," replied the President, ringing a little electric bell which was under his hand, "that we shall have to give you immediate proof of the earnestness of our intentions and our power to cause you a disadvantage."

At once four guards entered the room, whom Norman from their uniform and faces recognized to be the very palace guards who had let him and the supposed beggar pass into the palace the day of their memorable visit. Unfortunately for Norman, they wore no longer the air of benevolent sleepiness which had characterized them on that former occasion; they were obviously wide awake and attentive to command.

"Do you still refuse to perform the exercises demanded of you?" inquired the President.

"Yes," said Norman, stubbornly.

"Haul him up," said the President quietly, but with anger in his eyes.

Norman found his wrists seized before he could make the slightest resistance, and he was swung up on to the back of the tallest of the guards.

"Do you refuse also to apologize?" said the Doctor.

"Yes."

"Let him go away quietly," said the President.

"Why should we hurt him? We cannot expect him to understand us."

"I insist on an apology. I will not leave the room without it," said Norman. "As for you, you soppy little fool...."

His bewilderment rapidly gave place to alarm. He wished he had not been quite so rude to the President, who, after all, had been polite. Still, he hoped he might be simply undergoing some form of Test by Verification, like the legendary Masonic hot poker. At least, I suppose it is legendary. But when from the tail of his eye he beheld from his undignified perch a horsewhip in the hands of one of the guards, he tried to remember the sufferings of his days in the village school at Blaindon, which, after all, were not of such remote antiquity.

He wondered, like the schoolboy, how many? If, that is, he really was to suffer after all.

His apprehensions were confirmed and relieved by the President, who exclaimed in a wickedly gentle voice, "I'm very sorry, but I suppose you must give him a dozen." The maniac examiners were quite capable, he had felt convinced, of beating him to death, and a dozen? Why, a dozen was about the extent of the good old pedagogic punishments, which he had endured stolidly in his time, and many of them.

A new question surged through his mind. What was the brawny guard about to aim at? Was the supreme indignity to be conferred upon him before all these pompous personages to emphasize his unfitness for dignity? Norman hoped so, for to tell the truth, he didn't care a damn about the dignity, but he thought it would hurt less and was more used to it. Meantime he had never felt so cold, and the rough cloth of the guard who was holding his wrists so tightly grated unpleasantly against his naked chest.

His dignity was not damaged. His shoulders were. He discovered his old pedagogue to have been the mildest and most inefficient flagellator in the world. Let us leave him to his punishment and philosophize a little.

Philosophy and the whip? Is there not always some subtle connexion? Has not a whipping always meant for us something more than a whipping? Is it not a symbol? Think of this, youthful reader, if you are still in the happy days of subjection and possibility, and may it comfort you in the hour of trial. The Spartans formed their character, the Romans ruled the world, with whippings. With little whips the Kings of Egypt made the Jews work with their hands—honest manual toil, to which that race no longer much inclines; he built his pyramid and flogged a great nation into life. But the East, the golden East in the golden days—that was the world for whippings. In other climes and other times, whipping has been a symbol of degradation; in murderous Russia it has been, they say it is, something too foul for the philosopher to look at. But when there were Caliphs in Bagdad, then whipping was the joyous symbol of democracy. Are you rich and powerful, the Caliph's friend? Tread delicately on those rich carpets: the day comes when to put foot to the finest Bokhara may be a torment to make you howl. Are you a poor pedlar selling glasses from a tray? Repine not at your barefoot treading of the cobbled lanes: it is all practice for the soles; you shall fare better than your proud neighbour on the day of affliction. Quick! Bow your head: put your hands in the sleeves of your tattered abba. The great Vizier is coming, the Window of Heaven, the Tulip of the Garden of Government, the Sun's Moon, the Vizier. And behind him, O Allah! the blazing luminary of the universe itself! Where shall you hide from those dazzling rays? The Caliph comes. Some insolent retainer has kicked over all your glasses. Your little fortune has gone. No longer will you cry:

"O sunset, O sunrise, O ocean drops my glasses,
O emeralds, O rubies, O sapphires, O my glasses!"

Your wife will curse you, your children will starve; your dreams of a little ease are shattered with the shining crystals; your fortune lies with them prostrate in the dirt. You crouch in the doorway. But ho! what is that? The Vizier's horse has shied, he is kicking, he has kicked the Sun of the Universe off his saddle. All that splendour is smirching the bashful mud! Forgetting yourself, you rush to help him; your dirty, horny fingers pick up Perfection, careless of sacrilege. You wait and tremble, for Perfection is himself again. The Vizier is pale. The Monarch gives a sign to the blackest of his black negroes. Down comes the Tulip of the Garden of Government. The Vizierial beard is in the dirt; the Sun's Moon's feet are all in air and looped into a pole: the blows fall, the Tulip howls—and you? The Caliph has embraced you and made you Vizier on the spot. Such is a whipping in the East.

So much, then, for whipping from the point of view of historical geography. It has other aspects—too vast for mention here. The individual aspect, or the whippings inflicted on the famous, on Psyche by Venus, on Aristotle by Phyllis, on St Paul by the Romans, on-Henry Plantagenet by the monks, on Milton by his College, on Voltaire by a lackey, on Shelley by a schoolmaster. We read of the latter that he writhed on the floor not because he was hurt but out of shame. Ethereal Shelley!

Or take the literary aspect. Take the heroes of famous books—what whacks and thwacks they encounter, especially in all books that are an epitome of world life. From Apuleius to Don Quixote, from Gil Blas to Tom Jones, from Candide to Richard Feverel, there is no great book without its whipping.

And there are those who say children should not be whipped! They are right, dear youthful reader, they are entirely right. It is we who should be whipped, we adults, we pompous people, we who are so ready to torture the young and who have quite forgotten the bitterness of the torture we inflict. It is we who should be whipped, we who dread the dentist, we whose waistcoats bulge and blossom into gold watch chains. And criminals? O we flog them still, but only the poor, violent, rough fellow who does a bit of straightforward business. It is that fat financier whose juicy back I want to see streaked with red like a rasher of bacon; it is that ape-like vestryman whose yells would be music to my ears; it is, above all, the proprietor of pills that I would strap down to his alliterative and appropriate post, the pillory.

None of the above reflections occurred to Norman. His literary knowledge did not help him. He seemed to have spent whole years being whipped. He felt as if his lungs would burst. But the executioner laid on steadily and evenly, till the victim's back looked like a sheet of music paper. Then he was abruptly let down and writhed for half a minute with rapidly decreasing pain. And about this let the philosopher say one word more. Whipping is not strictly torture. It does not deform. It leaves no ill effects. And therefore many a parent who would shudder to use rack or thumb-screw to our children, think nothing of whipping them. But it need not hurt much less.

Norman, in absolute silence, put on his clothes. The examiners meanwhile filed out of the hall; the young shopman-president alone remained. For a mad moment Norman thought he saw tears in the President's eyes and pity in his face; but his own vision was dim, and certainly it seemed improbable that the brute who had ordered the whipping should be affected thereby to tears. When Norman was dressed the President said, "Follow me, I will let you out." Norman obeyed silently. They went alone together into the little shop. The boy had already begun to plot revenge, and now thought he saw his opportunity. Calculating the moment and the distance, he suddenly sprang like a tiger on the President. His effort was attended by no success. He found himself lying on the floor as swiftly as a skater who has tripped on a stone.

"Do you think I was not prepared?" said the President, smiling, as Norman picked himself up. And somehow, for all that his back was still aching, the charm and beauty of the young man, his soft voice and his insinuating smile, changed Norman's wrath into a sort of shame.

"So that's all I'm to get for coming with you," said Norman, like a rueful schoolboy. "You've forgotten even the present suitable for a lady."

"You're a wonderful person," muttered the President. "It's a pity we had to reject you." And opening a drawer he drew out a very beautiful jewelled clasp.

Norman muttered, "How much?" and felt in his pocket. He knew the receipts of Price's Bon Marché would not have paid for it in fifty years—if the stones were real.

"You have earned it this time," said the President, "and please not to take me for a shopkeeper again," and, opening the door into the street, he waited for Norman to go out. The boy hesitated.

"Tell me, to whom does all this belong?" he asked, voicing questions that troubled his mind. "And where is the Old Poet? And why did he choose me as a subject for his unpleasant jokes?"

"Good evening," said the President, pointedly. "I have nothing further to say to you but this, that if you say one word, one little word, to a soul of what has happened to-night—there are worse things awaiting for you than whipping." And with these ominous words he closed the door and shut Norman out into the street.

"This comes," said Norman, bitterly, "of following the advice of poets!"

CHAPTER IX

THE CONSUL

Again in the mist and shadow of sleep
He saw his native land.

The hero of this and all our adventures, feeling unheroic and disinclined for further traffic with his fellows, did not proceed to the board of the Widow Prasko, or to the no less hospitable embrace of her lovely daughter, but nursed revenge and a sore back by a walk on the walls. The path along the summit of these old fortifications is broad and smooth: it commands sea, mountains, town and all four corners of the heavens; many lovers, dreamers and successful suicides have passed that way. Yet surely it would need more than the vivid recollection of a sound thrashing to make a man leave such a prospect as that wall affords, especially westward, to the mountains and the setting sun. So Norman walked along the walls and not off them.

How to attain satisfaction? Whom to seek in this dilemma? How to be revenged and not ridiculed? How, above all, to get level with those lunatics without again being stripped and whipped like a schoolboy or enduring a worse thing, according to the strange young President's threat? What was the meaning of it, the sense of it, the clue to this mysterious and painful practical joke? Where, above all, was that ancient scoundrel of a poet and in what disguise, and why was he not present at the scene? Had the old curiosity shop been invented from the very beginning simply to attract him? How could they have known he would take the Poet's hint and look there for the present? How was it they were all prepared for him when he came? And, finally, what was the real value of the handsome buckle which he was to give Peronella? He pulled it out of his pocket: if the stones were real, and they looked it, he judged it to be worth a fabulous sum. For a moment he thought it might all have been a plot of Cesano's to befool him. But common sense soon rejected that theory: so artistic and elaborate a practical joke was far beyond the conception of that thin-brained cavalier. Norman walked twice round the walls in hopeless bewilderment, and longed to find a trusty soul to whom he could impart the whole affair. Then, as for the third time he faced the East, the sun of inspiration blazed full on the fields of his intellect.

Visions of Britain's might awake to protect her humblest subject rolled across his mind; of Dreadnoughts blackening the horizon, of a ten minutes' bombardment, of being hauled from prison by merry bluejackets pouring brandy down his throat, of shaking hands with a clean-shaven Admiral, of a protectorate over Alsander, and the immediate repaving of the roads and reconstruction of the sewers.

Was there no British Consulate in Alsander?

Comforted by a resolve to appeal to the might of Britain, he returned at once to the board of the Widow Prasko and the no less hospitable arms of her charming daughter. They had been quite anxious about him.

"And where is it?" was the girl's first question.

He pulled out the exquisite toy, and Peronella cooed with delight.

"My dear Peronella, it is far, far too good for you," said her mother, beaming with ostensible gratification, and burning to know whether any of the stones could possibly not be paste.

"Did you really find that in that poky little shop?" said Peronella.

"Oh, yes," said Norman. "It is a wonderful place, if you really only knew it."

"And look at that pattern round the border," said the observant widow. "How nicely it's worked, and so small."

"It is indeed," said the boy, examining it for the first time and turning a little pale.

This was the pattern:—\-AA-/: and it reminded him unpleasantly of the symbol he had seen that afternoon.

However, Norman, strong in his new imperial faith, went to his room, nearly cricked his neck examining the stripes in the mirror to see if they were still there and in good order for exhibition, turned in and slept.

Rising betimes the next morning he set out upon his quest. It was a long one, and the said new-born faith in the omnipotence of the British flag underwent a severe trial during this voyage of exploration, for some people seemed never to have heard of "British" and some never to have heard of "Consulate." Those who understood the meaning of these magic words in general failed to illuminate him in particular. Peronella and her mother belonged to this latter category, and so did most of the people he met in the street. At last he was informed in a draper's shop that it was down in a street off the Palace square. He arrived at the house indicated after a diligent and toilsome search and found it to let and uninhabited. He spent another half-hour scouring the cafes for the caretaker. The caretaker, having been plied with many drinks, directed him to a street off the Cathedral square at the other end of the town. Having arrived there, he discovered the street and the number. He found himself in front of a preposterously tall house in a state of violent ruin, which appeared about to fall on his head. It bore no outward consular sign at first glance, but by standing well back on the opposite side of the narrow street and craning his neck Norman could just discern what might be a coat-of-arms above a window on the top floor. He began the ascent of a staircase which deserved all the epithets usually applied to such staircases. He discovered during the long and intricate ascent that the house, or rather tower, contained a singular variety of inmates. On the ground floor was a shop where an extremely aged man with large spectacles was carefully affixing small bits of gold braid to form one of the gorgeous patterns which adorn the festal dress of Alsandrian beauty. The first floor was devoted to the offices of an insurance company, which Norman hoped had insured its own premises. On the second floor a photographer exhibited the terrifying results of his art. The contents of the third floor were to be judged from a show-case fixed on the wall in which whole mouthfuls of false teeth were symmetrically arranged. But the entrance to the fourth floor was guarded by a portal on which, by the aid of a match, Norman discovered bell-push and the gratifying legend, "British Consulate."

The door opened mechanically. "A very advanced door," thought Norman as he stepped in, "for this locality." He found himself in a small and neat office, at the first glance not remarkable. Afterwards he noticed, to his surprise, that it was full of contrivances, such as wires and switches and taps—something between a railway signal-box and the manager's bureau in a telephone exchange. Its only occupant was a thin man, with ruffled, mud-coloured hair, who was rattling on a typewriter with as much vigour as an amateur pianist thumping the presto of the "Moonlight."

"What do you want?" said the typist-clerk, very rapidly and sharply, in the tone of a vixenish and virtuous housewife accosted by blundering vice in a dark street.

"I should like to see the Consul," replied Norman.

"Why?" said the clerk, clicking on a new line and rattling off again.

"Even the British Consulate has gone mad in Alsander," thought Norman, in despair. "Or does he mean to be rude?"

"I have some urgent private affairs to discuss," he said.

"Passport?" urged the clerk.

"I'm afraid I haven't got one," said Norman.

"Name?" insisted the clerk.

"Price," snapped Norman, thankful it was monosyllabic.

The clerk seized a table telephone with one hand, while he still fumbled the keys with the other.

"Price—private—no passport," he shouted into the vulcanite ear.

"I must have come to the American Consulate by mistake," thought Norman, amazed at this un-British efficiency.

"In!" roared a voice into the telephone.

Norman could clearly hear it; it came from the next room.

The clerk pushed a button, the inner door opened, and Norman found himself in the presence of H.B.M. Consul,[1] Alsander.

The appearance of the Consul and his apartment, although peculiar, was the reverse of terrifying, as Norman was glad to find, after the mechanical horrors of the clerk's abode. In fact, it had hardly the appearance of a office at all. It was true the Consul was sitting at a large desk and wearing a very smart frockcoat, and that on the desk in conspicuous positions were volumes labelled Foreign Office Year Book, Circulars, Trade Reports, Miscellaneous, Shipping, Marriage Register, etc. But the walls of the room; presented a curiously unofficial appearance. They were papered with a thick-looking dull black paper, and ornamented with designs in black and white by Aubrey Beardsley. The carpet was a dull purple, indeed the room was in such harmony (except for the vivid letter-box red of the Foreign Office Year Book) that Norman felt his light-coloured waistcoat and pink cheeks to be unpardonable. The Consul himself was dressed with such a subtle lack of ostentation and was himself of such unostentatious appearance that Norman could not for a whole second discover him at all. At length he made out that the official had long drooping whiskers and was smoking a calabash and writing with his left hand, his right being apparently paralysed.

"Good morning," he said to Norman, in a very cheerful voice, rising to receive him.

"Forgive my left," he continued, cordially, as he extended that member. "A little accident, you know, Bulgarian bomb at Monastir, in the old days before the war. Compensation, you know. Well, then. However, there we are. Sit down. Take a chair. Or fill a pipe."

"I am so sorry to take up your time," said Norman, settling down in an all-black armchair and reaching out for a match.

"My dear sir," said the Consul. "I am delighted to see you. I may tell you I have been Consul in Alsander for two years and this is the first time I have received a visit in my official capacity. Have you"—his voice sunk into an expectative whisper—"have you a passport, signed and in order?"

"I am very much afraid," said Norman, "I neglected to get one."

"That is unfortunate, most unfortunate. But"—here his voice sunk to a guilty whisper "I might give you one. At all events, I assure you I am delighted to see you. Alsander is very slow, very slow, indeed."

"But you must be very busy," hazarded Norman. "I have never seen anyone so busy as your clerk."

"Ah, my dear sir, we must keep up appearances, you know. I let him think that I never have a moment to spare. I may tell you that I have been here two years and have not written an official letter since the day I announced my arrival. Such a change from Pernambuco, my previous post. There I never had a minute!"

"But he's typing like mad," said Norman, surprised, and quite unable to rid himself of the impression of the furious energy which had seemed to him to pervade the outer office.

A faint smile suffused the countenance of the Consul as he explained.

"Oh, I keep him employed, copying scraps of old blue books, you know, and that sort of thing. Might be useful some day."

"You must find life monotonous."

"Ah, yes. Such a change from Pernambuco. No casino, no theatre. The theatre at Pernambuco was delightful. This, you know, is one of our quietest posts. Even Archangel, where I was Vice-Consul twenty-three years ago, was a lot more lively. But I do not complain. The climate is good, the salary tolerable—poli kala, as I learnt to say in Patras."

"You have travelled, sir," said Norman, politely.

"Oh, one knocks about a bit and sees things in the Service. Hallo!"

The last ejaculation was not addressed to Norman, but to the telephone, whose bell was ringing violently.

"Let him wait," said the Consul.

"Perhaps," hazarded Norman, "if you are busy this morning I had better tell my story at once."

"Certainly. But you need not hurry at all. It's only Dr Sforelli come for his game of chess. You know him perhaps? You have heard of him only?... Yes, the report was correct; he is one of the ablest men in Alsander. His father's name was Cohen, by the way."

"Cohen Sforelli?" inquired Norman.

"Just Cohen," said the Consul. "Are you an Anti-Semite?"

"I never thought about it," said Norman, determined that he would begin his tale at all costs. "But I am Anti-Alsandrian at present."

"Been trying to sell something? Hallo, there! Let him wait. Only Olivarbo. You know Count Olivarbo? For an Alsandrian, a man of some ability."

"I hope he has not rung you up on urgent business."

"Oh, dear no. I am teaching him golf. Of course, I am a little handicapped"—he glanced pathetically at his limp member—"but the rules and the style, you know, and so on."

"Well, sir, if you don't mind, my business is rather serious, and I should like to come straight to the point. And to begin with, I should like to ask you whether you have heard of the Alsander Advancement Association."

"Never. Is it a co-operative store?"

"No, it purports to be a secret society, for the object—well, I don't know for what object."

"Of advancing Alsander?"

"I suppose so. But it seems to be really a conspirators' club to play bad practical jokes on innocent strangers. I was entrapped by one of its members."

"This is very interesting, very interesting, indeed. I may have to take a note of this. Hallo. Who's that? My dear Cocasso, I really can't this afternoon. I am being consulted on important business. Look up Cassolis, he plays. My dear sir"—this to Norman—"you were entrapped?"

"I was entrapped. The society sat in state and pretended to examine me for the position of King of Alsander."

"Well, well, why not? I was examined to become Vice-Consul. We must all be examined, you know."

"Yes, but that was not all. I was stripped and mauled about by a fool who pretended to be a doctor."

"Stripped? Dear me! Stripped naked?"

"Yes, but worse was in store for me. Because I demanded an apology for their nonsense, I was beaten."

"Beaten? Dear me! Beaten with a stick? Gracious heavens! Very extraordinary! I must make a note of that. And what would you like me to do?"

"Why, what do you usually do when a British subject is stripped and beaten by a lot of dirty Dagoes?"

"I do not remember such an occurrence; so I have no precedent for dealing with this case. British subjects do not usually expose themselves, you see, to such odd adventures."

"Do understand that it is serious, sir," pursued Norman, whose fury had been gradually mounting in face of this official apathy. "What's the good of being an Englishman if one can't travel unmolested? What's the good of all those Dreadnoughts? What are they wasting coal in the North Sea for? Why don't they come here?"

"I must remind you," said the Consul, severely, "that you have no passport. I cannot possibly send for the Fleet if you have no passport. For all I know you might be Siamese."

"Do I look it?" cried Norman, in dismay.

"Perhaps there are light-haired Siamese mountaineers who have learnt English from Indian friends. 'Quien Sabe?' as we said at Barcelona."

"It is a shame, sir—you are fooling me!" Norman's temper had quite gone.

"Have you only just found that out?" said the Consul, his eyes twinkling.

"I shall write to the Times," cried Norman, rising from his chair to leave.

"My brother," said the Consul, with a smile, "edits the correspondence columns of that august journal. Of course, he will print your letter. But he will also print"—here the Consul rose and his tone grew severer still—"a note to say that I treated you with all civility although you had no passport and no letter of introduction, and that you deceived me to my certain knowledge by telling half-truths."

"Half-truths!" exclaimed Norman.

"What about the jewelled buckle that was presented to you by the society?"

"Why, I had forgotten about it."

"And—a much more serious matter—what about the injunction to silence which was laid on you by the President?"

"You did not let me finish my story. What do you know about the jewelled buckle? How do you know there was an injunction to silence?"

"That injunction to silence you had better have obeyed, sir. However, you may rely on my discretion. If you insist on demanding reparation, I am bound to state your case before higher authorities, but I warn you you will get none, and you will endanger your life and perhaps mine. The present made to you was an ample reparation for your temporary inconvenience. I will give you a few minutes to consider the matter."

Norman sat down, bewildered. Before he could think of anything the telephone bell rang again.

"Come in," called the Consul. Norman rose politely as the newcomer entered.

"Mr Norman Price. Signor Arnolfo," said the Consul, introducing them.

Norman was about to shake hands, but his hand fell. Signor Arnolfo, a young man in the national costume, was the handsome President himself!

[1] I should perhaps mention that the Consul of Alsander bears not the slightest resemblance to any Consul in the Levant, Alsander being of course a much coveted retiring post in the General Consular Service.

CHAPTER X

CONTAINS THE PRESIDENT'S TALE AND A DEBATE ON THE ADVANTAGES OF MURDER

There was a fine contrast between the two boys as they stood confronting each other. They were both young, handsome, beardless. But Norman was square, strong jawed, with a hint of the workman about him; his hair almost silver, his blue eyes and fair complexion as British as could be. There was little to suggest anything more interesting than the handsome athlete about him save a fine, curious expression of the mouth, a bold forehead, and perhaps an exceptional regularity and symmetry of the features.

Arnolfo was in complete contrast: his whole body, though not well set off by the gorgeous but loose costume, seemed curiously slim and supple: his smooth, dark face had the spiritual beauty of the artist. No lack of determination in it, however, but the power was in the eyes rather than the chin, which was as softly rounded as a woman's. Of these eyes we can say but little; they were large dark eyes, but no poet can sing or painters paint the charms of the soul's windows. Even more beautiful was the mouth, on which hovered a smile. But though in the eyes of Arnolfo there shone a humorous sympathy, though his smile faded with obvious disappointment when Norman drew back his hand, Norman in his fury saw nothing but an insolent boy who had outraged him bitterly. Scorning with a flash of chivalry to use his fist on so frail a person, he nevertheless could not help administering to Arnolfo there and then a ringing smack on the cheek.

"How dare you, sir, commit an outrage on one of my friends in my presence?" The Consul's voice rang out severe and incisive.

"One of your friends!" cried Norman, almost hysterical with wrath. "What business has a British Consul with friends who outrage British subjects? I'd give you one, too," he added, savagely, "if it wasn't for your...."

"It is most impolite of you, sir," said the Consul, interrupting him and leaning across his desk, "to make any reference to the unfortunate state of my arm, due as it is, and as I have already hinted, to excessive zeal in the public service. Also, I may inform you, that you are quite welcome to go for me if you like. Your behaviour is uniformly gross. As for my infirmity, take that!"

And he dealt Norman across his desk a blow with the supposed withered arm which sent him reeling against the wall. Norman was about to reply to this onslaught in kind when Arnolfo interposed himself between them, his cheek still red from the blow.

"Remember," he said to the Consul, "he cannot understand and he has had a great deal to endure. I would think less of him if he had not hit me. Sir, I accept your blow. Will you cry quits with me and be friends?"

"You accept my blow indeed, you coward! I have given you a very good clout on the head. Why don't you challenge me to a duel like a man? Surely that is the custom everywhere outside England?"

"I will make you any reparation you like, but I will not fight you. Strange as it may seem, I hope that some day you may become my friend."

"Friend, indeed! You seem to credit me with outrageous generosity. If you are too frightened to fight, you must at least let me in my turn order you a sound thrashing. Then I can meet you on equal terms."

"Believe me, Signor Norman, I would do that for your friendship," said Arnolfo, and, turning to the Consul, he added, "Will you not leave me with this Englishman a minute?"

"I entreat you, Signor Arnolfo, you should not trust yourself to such a man. He is rude, unmannerly, and dangerous, and not at all likely to appreciate the refinement of your sentiments."

"I entreat you, do what I ask," said the young man, and as the Consul still seemed reluctant, he added in a whisper, "I command you." Upon this the Consul, bowing to Arnolfo, left them alone.

"Now, Signor Norman," began Arnolfo, "try and put aside for a moment your righteous and natural indignation. I have come on purpose to see you. I hastened here as soon as I was informed of your arrival. I want you to forgive me. I want you to be my friend. But, most of all, I want you to believe me to be sincere."

"How are you going to prove your sincerity to me this time?" inquired Norman. "By more subtle torture than beating or by downright murder? You and your friends have inflicted on me the most shameful degradation, and now you implore forgiveness and talk of sincerity. Are you, is this city, is the whole world, mad? Why should you want to talk to me about sincerity? Would it not be more to the point to discuss the figure of my damages?"

"Never be ashamed of your vulgarity, Mr Price," said the young man, without a trace of sarcasm in his gentle voice. "It gives you just that vitality which I have not got. It is exactly the absence of vulgarity from my character that makes me unfit to rule this kingdom alone."

"You seem to have no mean opinion of ourself. I know you only as a shopkeeper and as a conspirator. I agree with you that you are unfit to rule even this kingdom. Take at least the trouble to inform me who you are."

"Will you let me tell my story?"

"I have no interest in your story. But on condition that you have no further designs against me, I will listen to your narrative, provided it is short."

"Sir!" exclaimed Arnolfo, with a flash of passionate anger in his beautiful dark eyes, the genuineness of which not even Norman could doubt, but always speaking in the same gentle tone, "I have had enough of your British and barbarous sulkiness. I am the proudest man in Alsander, and I have let you strike me in the face. But I will not let you insult me further. Sit in that chair and listen to what I have to tell you. Remember now as then, here, as in the secret room of the conspirators, you are utterly in my power."

Norman, curiously stilled by these words, sank into the great armchair in silence. The black walls, the tortured pictures, the incense fragrance of the strange room—had the Consul journeyed to China also?—hypnotized his will. He felt tired and careless. He took almost a pleasure in obeying the elegant and frail young man, whose voice was as low as the music of distant waves.

"I," began Arnolfo, "am a nobleman of Alsander, to which I returned about a year ago, after an absence of many years in many civilized lands, especially in Ulmreich. My father is virtual ruler of the Court of the orphan Princess Ianthe, who (presuming that the present occupant of the throne dies incurably insane and childless) should one day be Queen of Alsander. My father, the Duke Arnolfo, as any peasant boy will tell you, is the guardian of the Princess. It was his plan that the Princess should be educated in Ulmreich, among a sober and wise people, where every facility would be obtainable to cultivate her mind and refine her intelligence. I will confess to you that it was his dream to seat a noble and wise woman on the throne of Alsander, even, if necessary, before the death, or at all events before the natural death, of King Andrea. Well he knows the miserable state of this little kingdom under the idle, foolish and cunning rule of old Count Vorza, and many a time he has only been restrained from riding into Alsander at the head of a handful of retainers and wresting the regency from Vorza by the thought of his young charge whose majority he, an unfortunate exile, has devoutly awaited.

"But, alas! nothing is likely to come of all his dreams. You may have heard flimsy rumours here to the effect that Princess Ianthe is as mad as her cousin. It is not quite true that she is mad. She is stubborn and unreasonable, and she is almost stupid. She grasps nothing, despite the most careful education that a woman could possibly receive. She has fits of piety and fits of melancholy. If that were all, married to a good husband, she might do passably well; but she has one supreme defect which makes her impossible as a queen. She is so ugly that it would be hard to find a man who would not be ashamed to be even so much as styled her husband, though the bribe were a crown.

"Carefully guarded as our little Court is, some rumours of the truth have come to Alsander, and at present Vorza seems to the popular estimation to be likely to go on ruling for ever. After all, the people are not unhappy: it is so many years since they have enjoyed the advantages of uncorrupt and energetic government they do not know that they are missing anything. But my father and I love Alsander with a burning passion; we dreamt of Florence, of Athens, of Venice, of the great deeds that have been performed by little States; and night after night we used to discuss what could be done with Alsander. We considered a republic, but a republic, even a small one, needs a dictator to tide over its growing pains and also a standard of education, which Alsandrians by no means possess. As for me, I knew myself to be incapable of governing Alsander alone, even had it been possible for me to acquire the supreme power by my father's influence."

(Norman, who had begun to listen with interest to the young man, and who had; thought that he was getting at the truth at last, noted in his mind the weakness of the last remark—coming from so self-confident young man. However, he did not interrupt, and Arnolfo went on.)

"It was decided finally that I should journey alone to Alsander, spy out the land, and attempt to form a conspiracy. It was a projects not without danger for myself. Vorza knows that the Court of Princess Ianthe is against him; my father warned me almost with tears against his treachery, and I could hardly persuade him to let me go. But once arrived in Alsander I put on so brave an outward show, played with such gaiety the part of an elegant young man bent on nothing but pleasure, that the suspicions of that crafty old fox were lulled with comparative ease. Cunning men seldom penetrate the cunning of others, especially the cunning of such others as have naturally no cunning in their nature, but are only playing a cunning part.

"In the meanwhile I made firm and loyal friends of all the really able or notable men in Alsander, to whom I carried letters of recommendation from my father. I found them surprisingly ready and willing to plot with me some change of government—but what change? I had deliberated long and in vain with several excellent people, when one day I was taken aside by Dr Sforelli, the King's physician, the very doctor to whose searching examination you so strongly objected the other day. He told me that there was a plot in the plot which now he would reveal. 'Your father,' he said, 'has partly deceived you. We are not groping in the dark; we have a plan already formed, a plan fantastic and wild, but still a plan; and we have cherished that plan for years. It was necessary that we should be assured of your discretion and ability before inaugurating our conspiracy; yet we postponed our action in order to await your intelligent co-operation, and, above all, in order to fulfil your father's dearest wish, which was that you should in person preside over the work of the regeneration of Alsander. Our plot is based on a very startling and curious fact, which is this—that practically from and including the day of his coronation not a soul in Alsander, not even Vorza, who is afraid of lunatics—has set eyes on King Andrea.'

"I expressed my astonishment.

"'This extraordinary state of affairs, though based originally on pure chance, is by no means accidental,' explained Sforelli, continuing. 'It was all arranged between your father and myself years ago. It had been actually necessary to seclude the King for a time, and your father, seized by a sudden and wonderful inspiration, gave me the word to convert the temporary seclusion into a permanent one.'

"'That is an extraordinary state of affairs,' I remarked, 'but I do not see how it will help in the regeneration of Alsander.'

"'Think!' said the Doctor, with his queer Jewish smile, and then the whole scheme dawned on me."

"Ah," said Norman, who had forgotten all his animosity in his interest in this amazing tale. "That was a superb idea. Of course, if no one has ever seen the King, you can substitute anyone you like and pretend the madness has been cured, without any revolution, bloodshed or fuss."

"Precisely, sir; but not quite anyone we like. Anyone outside Alsander. Anyone the people do not know. Anyone who is worth substituting. We had to find a ruler, and we set seriously about the task of discovering one. The Doctor had sent friends of his as emissaries to every land, like the Oriental Kings who desired husbands for their daughters and heirs for their crowns, to find a man fit to rule the kingdom. But our emissaries had a more difficult task than those of the Oriental potentates. They had first of all to find a man suitable—and though all that is needed, after all, is a certain amount of honesty, energy and intelligence, for it's not so hard to manage a little State like ours, yet we soon discovered that most honest, intelligent and energetic men were, unfortunately for our purpose, already installed in worldly positions so enviable that they were not likely to leave them for a chance of ruling a miserable country and an off-chance of being killed. Besides, the prospective candidates for royalty could not be trusted with the secret. The honest men might come to think it consistent with their honesty to betray the scheme. The proposed Bang would have to be tempted to Alsander, and, once there, most cautiously treated. And the emissaries the Doctor could send were very few, and poor.

"There was only one of them who was sanguine of success. He was an old man, an English poet...."

"Ah!" interjaculated Norman.

"... He had lived for many years, apparently without means of subsistence, in a broken attic, where he said he was composing a great Ode to the Sun. Sforelli, it seems, knew the old man well, and often declared to incredulous company that the supposed old imbecile was the most intelligent man in Alsander and perhaps in England. The Old Poet, as I said, swore he would succeed."

"Ah!" said Norman, "he has failed!"

"He has not failed," said Arnolfo, rising and laying his hands on Norman's shoulder. "He found you selling biscuits in an English village, and he swears that his feet were pulled to the village against his will at least seven miles on a hot summer afternoon, and all by the power of the Jinn! And now, though we feigned to reject you yesterday, you are the man we are going to make King of Alsander. And if we have to torture you into acceptance, King of Alsander you shall be."

Gently pronouncing the strange threat, the boy stood over Norman and looked down into his face and smiled. The world went unreal for Norman at that moment: he wondered if he were alive.

"I cannot believe a word of it," Norman said slowly, after a time. "But, no, I cannot! If you really wanted a man to rule this country—let us not say a King—it sounds too foolish—you would not choose an English grocer, examine his flesh as though he were a prize pig, thrash him before the eyes of his future subjects, and drive him out like a dog?"

"It was really necessary to see the physique of the man who is to found a dynasty. I fear, though, the Doctor took his duties himself too seriously. I fear, too, the whimsicality of the situation got hold of us: we were inclined to make the most of it. It is not every day one examines a man for the post of King. And as for the rest—we had to frighten you—into secrecy, and if possible into a belief if not of our sincerity at least of our power. We had to be able to command your silence, and it was obvious you were not ready to believe our good faith."

"Then show me your good faith!" rejoined Norman. "Surely I have a right to demand that? I only claim the just equivalent—that I should deal with you as you dealt with me."

"Ah, you do not know," said Arnolfo, paling, "what you ask of me. On the day I make you Bang you may do with me what you will—I promise you. You will rule me then; but I could not accept the dishonour from you now. If you think me a coward—I am a coward, but I can overcome my cowardice. That is not my reason," the boy went on, holding out his hands to Norman with a wan smile. "There—take my hands—torment me as you will; but not till the day you are crowned in the Cathedral of Alsander shall you have your full revenge."

Norman rose and took the delicate hand, and shook hands with a smile. "I cannot help it," he said. "I do not care if you want to make me your jest again, or if you want to kill me, but I am yours to command. I can even forgive you. But as for your plan it is plainly impossible."

"I think I do not care if it is, so long as I have your friendship," said Arnolfo, with strange warmth. "However, I admit there are many difficulties and many dangers in our plot, but what are those that strike you specially?"

"Do I look like an Alsandrian, first of all! Or must I be made up to look like one?"

"Heavens, we will not stoop to disguise. Besides, I have a touch of the artist, sir, in my composition, and never would I have your features altered, your colour changed, or a hair of your head displaced. In any case, the Royal Family were always fair. Kradenda was a Viking. Remember, also, you have only to deceive the ignorant mob. All the intelligent men of Alsander are in the plot."

"But I have been here for weeks!" objected Norman. "Every one knows me as the mad Englishman."

"You have been playing Haroun Al Rashid, and spending the first days of your return to Alsander spying out the land. It is a very pretty story, and will greatly enhance your popularity. Besides, the Old Poet instructed you to weave a mystery round your movements, and I learn from a sure source that you obeyed him."

"Then all this they tell me," gasped Norman, "that the King was sent abroad to be cured was got up on purpose for the plot?"

"Of course, and the announcement that his return and his cure are expected. Not a detail has been forgotten by Sforelli. There were guards at the palace, a closed carriage, a special train."

"And the Consul?" gasped Norman.

"The Consul is an agent of the British Government, and the British Government, tired of wanting a strong Turkey, happens at this moment to want a strong Alsander."

"And Vorza?"

"Vorza is a fool," said the young man, but with less conviction than usual.

"And the King himself. What shall we do with him?" pursued Norman.

"What of him? One of the guards knows of a little tap invented by the Japanese, as simple as the Jiu-jitsu trick with which I felled you in the shop the other day. The King really is the last person to be considered."

"But, really, if you want me to have anything to do with it," cried Norman, in horror, "I cannot touch murder."

"Not murder, but removal. What use is the poor devil's life to him or to the world?" So saying, Arnolfo sat down in the armchair facing his interlocutor and eyed him with interest.

"I am not an Alsandrian. In England we view these things differently," said Norman, pompously, shocked that his gentle companion should be capable of designing such an atrocious outrage. But Arnolfo answered unperturbed:

"In England I believe on one occasion you gave a King a mock trial and then beheaded him under circumstances of inconceivable barbarity. Ah! you're an Englishman, and mad like all of them, as mad as Andrea. Come, I love argument; let's have it out. One life, one rotten, miserable life to buy the happiness of a country, and you won't spend it. You call it principle. When you go to war, what do you care for life? You are not religious in the matter. It's just that fetish you call law. I did not ask you to kill the imbecile yourself; it will be done quietly."

"I will have nothing to do with any filthy, cold-blooded murder. It isn't fetish: it's simply because I won't."

"And if we deal with you instead of with him?"

"Try. I do not like your cynicism."

"I am sorry. But it is unreason on your part, or else sheer cowardice. By what code of ethics in the world do you justify yourself? You are just frightened to do something that would make your conscience uncomfortable. On what do you base your morality?"

"On feeling."

"Would your feelings let you kill a man who was just going to kill some one else?"

"Certainly."

"Then why not a man whose existence does harm to others?"

"Others might think my existence did harm to them."

"But a life that is worthless to itself?"

"May not the poor fool's life be happier than yours or mine?" said Norman, who was always fond of abstract argument and apt to grow eloquent in the realm of ideas. "He lives with his ideal. His cobwebbed, cracked-plaster room is for him a most elegant palace; he sees the phantom courtiers all day long; they bring him presents of fruits and flowers and spices and gold. He is for himself the great Emperor of the World, for all we know."

"Then you will not justify a political assassination?"

"No. It's not so easy as you think, nor are my reasons so trumpery, Arnolfo—for you're as shallow as you are clever. Murder cuts at the source of all society—which war, which is organized killing, does not. Unorganized killing means death not to one man here or there but to society. That is why we English, who think society a good thing, hate murder. Let it loose, unpunished, and if but twenty people are killed the law unheeding, it's worse for society than if twenty thousand perish in war or plague. I will not touch it."

"Your reasoning is powerful, Norman, but it's not your reason that influences your action. Your act is, as you said before, in accordance with your feelings. I might combat your reason, but I cannot change your convictions. What can we do?"

"Well, it's not so terribly urgent to get rid of him."

"What can possibly be done with him?"

"Why, send him to a lunatic asylum, of course."

"What a ghastly piece of perverted common sense. O, you Englishmen; you have never realized that the French Revolution has occurred. You are still a hundred years behind the Continent. But I am Alsandrian, my friend, I am Southern; I have all the Southern weakness."

"And some of the Southern charm," added Norman. Though he had recovered under the stress of the ethical argument from the hypnotic fascination to which he had succumbed, he began to be not so sure that he did not like this strange and gracious person.

"But none of the Southern faithlessness," Arnolfo rejoined. "Trust me, Norman. Trust me and I will be faithful to you to death. I—we all of us need you so desperately. This about the murder was only nonsense—to hear what you had to say, though I'm afraid the good Sforelli suggested it in earnest. There is good work, man's work, an Englishman's work to be done here. Once the fantastic stuff—the mummery—is over, you may achieve true greatness."

"I shall become a thief," said Norman. "Do you want to argue that?"

"You are right to remember it. That repugnance you must sacrifice: you are going to seize an all but worthless property and make it fine land for corn and olive."

"Yet what I said of murder applies to theft: I am helping to cut at the basis of society."

"But to found a new one. Come, in this objection you will not persist. You have not the same emotion, you do not really mind."

"Or, rather, you wake in me such emotions—such schoolboy emotions—that I cannot control them. It's a game—but it's worth playing. I don't care what awaits me—discovery-disaster—death! I don't care if you're fooling me. I follow you, Arnolfo. What are your orders?"

"Continue to play the part the Poet assigned to you, that is all. Hint of the mystery. I will prepare the rest as quickly as I can. About the King, I will arrange something to please you. And now, good-bye."

Norman held out his hand, but Arnolfo, under the stress of subdued emotion, laid his hands on Norman's shoulders and kissed him.

"A Southern way," he said, half laughing, half ashamed. "One more thing, remember, I had almost forgotten," he added, as he opened the door for Norman. "That is, beware of women."

CHAPTER XI

A VISIT TO VORZA

"Norman, you must be awfully rich."

So the guileless Peronella to him on his return, breathlessly emerging from the room to greet him.

"Have you only just found that out?" said Norman, assuming the slight modest smile of a man who has been hiding his infinite superiority.

"Yes. Why, of course, the buckle you gave me was very beautiful, but I had no idea.... I put it on this morning and went for a walk in it, and all the jewellers came running out of their shops to praise it and ask about it and offered thousands of francs for it. And, O Norman, I wouldn't sell your buckle for anything, but if you would get me one of those lovely big hats the Frenchwoman sells in the High Street, just to go with it."

"You are much finer as you are, my lass, with a kerchief round your head."

"Oh, but do, Norman, dear! It seems that buckle of yours is worth enough to buy a new hat for every girl in Alsander."

Norman was about to surrender when he suddenly remembered he had rather less than a napoleon left in the world. "Well, I am in a foolish fix," thought he. "If I don't follow up the buckle, I shall be accused of having stolen it." (He surmised correctly; Alsandrian cunning was already suspicious of him.) "And my clothes are dreadful: a millionaire or Prince, even in disguise, would not wear shiny blue trousers: a Prince in rags is all right, but not a Prince in bags. I wish I had given a hint to that marvellous Arnolfo, but somehow I expected him to know everything without being told. And perhaps it was all a dream and he a phantom."

So he shut himself up in his room for the rest of the day.

"I have important letters to write," he said, impassively. "You must be content with the buckle, Peronella. Wait a little while, and I'll dress you in gold from head to foot."

He retired, not to write, but to think and meditate. He had supper in his room, and for the first time in his life disliked cabbages. Then he went to bed. As he was falling asleep he wondered whether he had not been raving in his mind for the last few days: whether he was not being fooled: whether he would succeed, what he would do when a King. There was plenty to do: the town was very dirty. An ecstatic vision of having all the drains up flitted across his mind. Succeeded a vision of fine mountain roads with cunning wriggles, and the royal motor car sliding up them. Then the vision of a Court ball with more-than-Oriental splendour. Then the perplexing vision of a little fool of a girl, damned pleasant to see and touch, crying her stupid heart out.

However, he slept. He was awakened by a scrubby postman, who handed him a registered letter. Norman opened it hastily, and was delighted to find that it contained English banknotes for a hundred pounds—delighted but not surprised, for Arnolfo had by now deadened his sense of wonder. He gave the postman twopence, and had breakfast in bed on the strength of his opulence. Indeed he rose so late that at the bank to which he directed his footsteps a five-pound note was changed only with the greatest reluctance, five minutes before noon, the Alsandrian closing time. However, after a lot of little sums had been worked out by a lot of little desks and after the five-pound note had been bitten, crackled and held up to the light, and after Norman had executed a lot of complicated moves and marked time strenuously in front of grilled windows and "caisses" (all Continental banks seem to work on the supposition that you have come there to pass a forgery or rob the till), he was released with a large number of silver coins bulging in his trouser pockets.

He stood for a moment on the threshold blinking at the sun, his contentment tempered by annoyance at the reflection that all the shops were closed and would not be opened again for another three hours, so that he could not buy so much as a pocket handkerchief for his personal adornment, when he heard a whirring clangorousness, and there appeared a motor car crawling and puffing along the ruinous cobbles, followed by a little crowd of admirers, for a motor was as strange in Alsander as an aeroplane (shall I add "a year ago"?) above Upper Tooting. Norman would have known that the car was a London taxi had he ever been to London. The driver, smartly uniformed, stopped opposite him, and Arnolfo dressed in his invariable silk and gold stepped out, and bowed to Norman with a very ostensible deference. "I hope, Sir," he said suavely, "you will do me the honour of stepping into my car and coming to lunch with me at a little place I know of?"

"Why, how did you find me here?" cried Norman. "You are as bewildering as the Cheshire cat."

"It's not hard to find a suspicious fellow like you in a gossipy town like Alsander!" laughed Arnolfo. "Some other day, moreover, you shall tell me who the Cheshire cat was; but jump in now; we have no time to lose."

"I ought to hesitate," said Norman, but he stepped in at once.

"We are going to continue playacting on the lines laid down by the Poet," said Arnolfo, as soon as they were ensconced in the car and being jolted softly and slowly over the atrocious roads. "But you must forsake the proletariat for the aristocracy, and therefore I am going to take you round the town after lunch and dress you up like a Jew on a racecourse. For your story is to be that you are a rich English nobleman (any eccentricity will be swallowed in Alsander if you say you are a rich English nobleman), but that you find that you have Alsandrian blood on your mother's side from the fifteenth century. You see, the story you must tell at present should be a suspicious and extraordinary one, as you are soon going to disavow it when you proclaim yourself King: nevertheless it ought not to be so foolish as to be instantly found out."

Arnolfo continued to explain in great detail, as the car bumped gently on, the exact coat of arms, the exact relationship, the name of the Alsandrian family (a cadet of which had actually disappeared in England in the wars) and various other minute details.

When the car stopped they descended, and entered a curious and neat restaurant of which they seemed to be the only habitues, for it had only one table: there they had an excellent meal. Norman would have sworn it was a private house had not Arnolfo paid the bill and tipped the waiter. He would have sworn correctly, for it was. They then drove to a tailor, a haberdasher, a shoemaker, a hatter, at all of which places Arnolfo took the shopman aside and whispered that the order was for a very distinguished English nobleman, and should be executed without delay. Sometimes he would also let drop as a confidential favour that the nobleman "havas sango Alsandra en la venai," or that "Milord had come to dwell in the country of his ancestors." The Grand Tour Englishman of fabulous wealth and high distinction remained traditional in Alsander, since the Polytechnic Englishman, neither wealthy, nor distinguished, nor fabulous, had not yet arrived; and an Englishman with Alsandrian blood was a prize for the avaricious.

Norman was ostentatiously deposited at his garden door by the car, and for the rest of the day refused to answer any questions, and remained suggestive, impressive, mysterious and aloof, to the great discomposure of the Widow Prasko and her daughter. Cesano came in (I think by the widow's invitation, who hoped to inflame the obviously cooling Englishman with jealousy), but Norman offered no remonstrance to his taking Peronella for a walk. (Not that Cesano had much joy of the moonlight: the girl was moody and returned I to cry herself to sleep within the hour.) Our hero then had to fly before the onset of the widow, who told him—so closely does Alsandrian correspond to English idiom—that he owed it to her, positively owed it to her, to reveal his identity and regularize his position.

"Give me a week," said Norman, shuffling away from her and feeling more like a grocer and less like a King every instant.

As he undressed before the tarnished mirror the marks of the whip, which still stood clear across his back, seemed to rebuke his conceit; his dreams, too, were more humble; he dreamt he was married to the Widow Prasko and kept a boarding-house at Margate.

The next morning a messenger, who looked preposterously discreet, brought a letter from Arnolfo, making an appointment at the British Consulate, and certain ready-made clothes which, as a temporary measure, had been skilfully and swiftly adapted to his form.

Norman at the hour of his appointment found himself once more ensconced in the great armchair in the Consul's black-papered study, listening to Arnolfo. The Consul was not present.

"We have a difficult and dreary task on hand to-day," Arnolfo began. "I am going to take you to visit all the important people of Alsander. We will take Sforelli with us in order to make our movements look suspicious on recapitulation. It will be much more natural for you to become King if you have already obviously moved in aristocratic circles. Your few weeks among the people will be readily credited provided that it is known that you came afterwards to visit the upper classes as well. Some of those whom we shall visit are in the secret: but we have not entrusted the secret to their wives. Some of them may be clever enough to guess that you really are the King; indeed, we are going to spread a few hints to that effect: it will pave the way for future demands on the credulity of Alsander. Of course (as I have already hinted) the presence of the Doctor as your companion will be looked upon as remarkable and invite the sort of comment we desire.

"Remember, Norman, to be most distinguished—and at times a little strange. You are, so to speak, paying official visits incognito. And the last visit we shall pay will be to Count Vorza. O beware of that man: he is a fool as I said before—but he is a clever fool. Come, let us be going!"

"But surely," exclaimed Norman with a glance at Arnolfo's magnificent attire, flashing at the side of his dark frockcoat, "you cannot call on the best people in that costume!"

"Can I not!" replied Arnolfo as they descended the interminable stairs. "There is a tradition in Alsander which it is at once unusual, distinguished and meritorious to preserve, that the Alsandrian national costume lis sufficient and full dress for any Alsandrian or any occasion."

Sforelli was waiting for them in the car, and they went motoring round together to the Papal Legate, the bank manager, nobles, consuls—there was not even a minister in Alsander—and so forth. Norman, chiefly by preserving as far as possible a discreet silence, did well, and was complimented by Arnolfo.

"The ladies thought you most distinguished, my friend," he said. "But you have now the harder task I told you of. There is the gate of Vorza's city mansion. Once more, beware! What men say of the old man is true. The aged reactionary is as polite as an Italian and as cunning, as treacherous and as wicked as Abdul Hamid the Turk. So be careful."

It was a needful warning. The old man, very picturesque in his velvet skull cap, received them with great cordiality, and having expressed his great friendship for all Englishmen and referred half-a-dozen to a dozen times to the fact that he had been to London for three days in his youth, contrived that his wife, a colourless person, should take away Arnolfo and Sforelli to a recess and show them photographs. He thereby had a chance of seeing Norman alone, and extracting as much information from him as possible without the intervention of his companions.

"I am always so delighted to meet an Englishman," began the old minister, as soon as they were both ensconced in comfortable chairs, "especially as I have been to London myself. It is true I was there only for a short time, and that many years ago—you see I am old—but I have a vivid memory of it all. I remember the policemen—marvellous! But we see very few Englishmen here. May I ask how you came here, or was it just that curiosity of Englishmen that always drives them round the world? But you speak Alsandrian and between us I have even heard that you have a touch of the Alsandrian in you?"

"It is the attraction of my blood that brought me here, undoubtedly. I have a great interest in my ancestry."

"But you are obviously all English. You cannot have much Alsandrian blood. Tell me of what family you are. Between us—I know all the families in Alsander."

Norman endured the most searching scrutiny with regard to his ancestry. He made hardly a mistake. There was little that Vorza did not know about the old families of Alsander.

"Really," he said, genially, "your visit is as interesting as it is delightful. The visit of an English nobleman to Alsander is not an everyday occurrence. Your visit to the common people and interest in their daily life—that was most characteristically English of you. Yes, your visit, sir, is a great surprise and it coincides with another surprise for us Alsandrians. You know events are rare here, but this will be a great one."

"You mean the cure of the King?"

"Yes. I don't believe it. Sforelli, you know one of those Jews, between us—just a little bit too clever! Wonderful how he picked you up: I should drop him if I were you, by the way. And I had always heard that his poor Majesty was quite, quite mad. I never went to see. I dislike madmen as much as Jews. Arnolfo should not have introduced you to Sforelli, but the boy is so kind to every one! And I'm sure the King cannot be quite recovered—there will be something a little wrong. And a relapse—what a tragedy! Of course, I shall be delighted. I am an old man, and (between us) tired of ruling a thankless country. It would have been too long to wait for the Princess to grow up: now she'll be out of it, poor girl!"

"Which Princess?" interjaculated Norman, innocently.

"Don't you know? His Majesty's cousin, the heir to the throne. She lives with her mother's family far away in Ulmreich. They say she is mad also, and there is no holding her. Old blood, old blood! She was to have come here this year to be introduced to Alsander, but the idea fell through till the possibility of the King's cure had been established one way or another. I have not seen her since she was a girl. She is under the guardianship of the father of that charming young man, your friend Arnolfo. I am sorry I shall not be able to see her again."

"Bring her here and marry her to her cousin," said Norman.

He was quite detached at the time from all thought of his plot.

"A very good idea. But I don't know," replied the old man. "Between us, two mad people! Would it be good for the future of Alsander?"

"You are fond of the country?" inquired Norman.

"Passionately. I love its beauty. Between us, I want it just to remain as it is—a lovely and peaceable place, untouched by the world."

"You don't believe in progress?"

"Not for Alsander. They want me to repair the roads. Never, said I. Saving your friend's presence, I hate automobiles. They would soon be roaring all over the country and spoiling it absolutely. Our roads were made for carts and mules: and the people are quite happy with them. Your friend has one: just as a curiosity, it doesn't matter. Your friend," he added in a low voice, "was an infant when I last saw him before his return to Alsander. I knew his father years ago. A delightful man, but of advanced views. Now, Monsieur Arnolfo has no views at all, but almost anything can be forgiven him for keeping up the old traditions of the national costume, and he's a great acquisition to our little society. Between us, have you known him long?"

"I? No. I should very much like to know more of him. I brought a letter of introduction to him from a relative in England, who had met him and his father in Ulmreich. As you said, he is charming: there is no other word."

"Is he not? Charming: of course restless, but not like his father, who couldn't live in Alsander because it was what he called reactionary. Oh, if his father, old Arnolfo, got a chance, he'd run a funicular up the mountains and build a casino on the beach."

"Well, there's something to be said for being awake and something to be said for modernity," observed Norman.

"True, sir, but (between us)," said Vorza, with a more confidential tone than ever, "I have been, I admit, only a very short time in England, three days, in fact; and I am a bit of a judge, perhaps, in matters of taste—and I didn't see anything in London, among your latest buildings, at all events, that quite comes up to our Cathedral or our Castle."

"But your Cathedral and Castle weren't built by a people fast asleep, but by a people who had just awakened. If Kradenda had lived to-day he would have established an aeroplane service across the mountains.

"Well, well, and would we be happier for that? Ah, you're young and you're English, and I wouldn't think much of you if you weren't for all things new. At your age I was the devil! I may be more foolish now, but we old men want to think we have grown wise."

"You want to sift the question, Excellency; but that's a long, long matter. Perhaps happiness is not the best thing in the world. But here is Arnolfo."

And they took their leave.

"Curses!" said Vorza to himself, as he watched their departure from the window. "Ten million curses. Is this a surprise return? Is it the King? It's about the age. But he looks too British, too British altogether. But, then, so did his grandfather. There's not much madness in his eyes or talk. It cannot be. He might be cured, but he could not be intelligent. And that physique—it's impossible. But there's something up. Why did I trust Sforelli? In the old days I would have burnt him, gaberdine and all! Curses on him, at all events, and on me! How am I to know whether he is the King or no? If it's a plot—it may succeed—it is so simple. Perbacco! how simple it is! Well, we shall see!"

CHAPTER XII

IN WHICH THE BEETLES CRAWL

But solid beetles crawled about
The chilly hearth and naked floor.
James Thompson, author of the "City of Dreadful Night," popularly ascribed to Mr Kipling.

All preparations for this most surprising conspiracy were to be ready, so Arnolfo gave Norman to understand, on the following afternoon, and Norman, doubting his senses and still doubting the seriousness of Arnolfo, rose early and came to the appointed place, which was again the British Consulate, before the appointed time. After a few minutes there came to greet him, not Arnolfo, but Sforelli, a gentleman who would have looked heroic in a burnoose beside the ruins of Palmyra, but seemed merely intellectual and rather repulsive in a morning coat. He handed Norman a letter sealed with what Norman knew to be Arnolfo's seal. It ran as follows:

"DEAR NORMAN,—

"Everything is going well. Please put yourself entirely in the hands of Dr Sforelli, the bearer of this, who has full instructions from the Society. I am so busy, I may not see you again till you are crowned.

"ARNOLFO."

Norman, looking at the Palestinian profile before him, felt that the spring had left the year. The gay youth, with his wit and plots and disguises, would make anyone believe or even do anything. While this worthy? The transition from Greece eastwards was overpowering.

Yet one could see this swarthy, powerful person was to be trusted, more to be trusted than Arnolfo. Norman burst into a flood of practical questions.

"We shall just walk there," came the answer to Norman's first batch of inquiries. "I often go to the palace, as I live quite near, in the square: I have a dissecting room there: my wife objects to having corpses in the house."

"Dissecting? In Alsander?"

"Yes," replied the doctor, in hollow tones. "It was expensive getting corpses in pickle from Paris. So I advertised in the Centjaro, the little local paper you may have seen, the one that hints so broadly that the King of Alsander is already in the town incognito."

"But with success? Surely, in such a religious country...."

"There was money offered," continued Sforelli, dryly. "My door was besieged. I am not sure I was not responsible for murder, even for parricide. Some of those whose near relations were rejected went away in tears."

"Well, Doctor Sforelli, to the point. This mad central idea you are sure of—that no one has seen the King; but what about the guards?"

"The guards are with us."

"But why should they be with us?"

"They are sensible men, for one thing. They are very old servants of Arnolfo's, for another."

"Then Vorza?"

"He has never seen the King, you know that already."

"And the other notables?"

"All the members of the Town Council, which is the progressive element in Alsander, are with us. For all that, none of them have seen Andrea."

"But has there been no ceremony? For instance, was Andrea never crowned?"

"Yes, but with little pomp. There was only the Bishop there and myself. He was crowned in the empty room."

"And the Bishop?"

"Is fortunately dead. No one lives but myself who saw that mock coronation and a small acolyte who is now one of the most able young men of our party. The people were kept outside, but I remember they applauded, none the less. But the only person who was really impressed was the King himself. It meant a great deal to him, that shabby ceremonial!"

"What has given the King that antique form of speech?" pursued Norman.

"Before his mind left him, he had as a boy read one book—that of Makso."

"A! a great book!" cried Norman. "There is real fire in his tales of chivalry."

"And poetry, too," added Sforelli, "of no inconsiderable merit. Well, you know how the greatness of Kradenda is ever being sung therein. And ever since the boy, as he has heard but little human speech about him, has had faint echoes of the immortal language of Makso trickling through his brain."

"One hardly realized he was so young," said Norman, with a sudden pity.

"He is your age," replied Sforelli.

"Is there no hope of cure?"

"None," said the doctor, decisively. "None—on my professional honour. His delusions come from mental weakness, not from aberration. I might cure a man who had wandered from the road of reason, but not one who has never taken it."

So saying they started for the palace, on foot as Sforelli advised, to attract less attention.

"You are still determined not to have Andrea killed?" inquired Sforelli.

"That I prohibit absolutely," said Norman, speaking with authority for the first time.

Sforelli bowed with some irony.

"Fortunately," he said, "there is a small asylum outside the town under my supervision."

"How are we to get him there?" pursued Norman.

"I think of drugging him, and then driving him there myself to-night. It will not be difficult."

"I have your word, you intend to do this, and to do no more than drug him?"

"Although I consider that this humanitarian project of yours is fraught with great danger to our plans, you may trust me," said Sforelli, quietly, and Norman believed the man could be trusted for all his antipathetic ugliness. He inquired:

"And what am I to do while you do this?"

"I am afraid the safest plan will be for you to stay alone in the castle overnight pending my return. It may be rather disagreeable and lonely for you, especially as you may naturally feel nervous on the eve of our great coup, but I see nothing else for it. I must take the King to the asylum myself. It is not safe that any of our friends should either take charge of the madman or bear you company in the castle, for obvious reasons. I cannot be back much before dawn. When I return I shall send an official note to Vorza and explain, by your royal request, that the young 'English nobleman' who visited him the other day is none other than the cured Bang of Alsander. I shall add that you have returned to the Palace and desire to have the news kept secret for the present except from him and a few other notables. I shall further explain that you desired to remain a few days incognito in Alsander from a natural desire of seeing things as they are.

"You will send, written in your own hand, at the same time a command to your well beloved and trusted servant Count Vorza to appear at such an hour, and similar intimations (though not in your Royal hand), together with injunctions to secrecy, will be sent to other notables of Alsander. This letter will be sealed by you with the Royal seal of Alsander, which is in my possession.

"When the time comes you will have to play your part with the utmost care and even if you recognize some of the visitors as being members of the society and fellow conspirators, do not cease acting for a moment. I will tell you the story to which you must hold and to which you must, so to speak, mentally refer when in difficulty. I will tell it you to-morrow morning, when I return, in the palace, in great detail, so that your memory will be fresh for the day. But for the present, so as to get your mind accustomed to it, note that its outline is roughly this: You have been cured in England, mind you, and your mind is almost a blank for everything before that, save that you have vague reminiscences of Makso's poems, and a father and a mother. You had an operation—trepanning. And so forth."

"But it's too unconvincing scientifically. Scientists are sure to arrive and ask questions."

"Scientifically it will be as correct as a story by your own Mr Wells, when I have given you all the details. And I will answer the scientists myself. Above all, avoid being too explanatory. Nothing causes suspicion to arise so much as the volunteering of convincing information."

Thus conversing they arrived at the palace gate. It was already dark and not a soul stirred in the palace square. Two guards saluted them at the doorway. Norman recognized one with a shudder and one with surprise. One was the flagellator, the other the overworked clerk from the British Consulate. Two further guards, rising from their seats on the inner side of the gate, followed them in silence across the moonlit garden. The jasmine was fragrant. The doctor opened a little door. Norman passed once again into the curious corridor, and thence into the throne-room. It was lit by many candles, and was very hot. Everything was there as on his last visit—plaster cupids, broken divans, singeries, the old chair of Kradenda, and the madman looking as unreal as his surroundings—a part of the fantastic picture—glimmering in the dim light. The King, however, though still robed in ermine and cloth of gold, was without his crown, and there was one further change. Everything, except the King, had been washed. Even by the faint illumination this was perceptible. The candelabra shone, the fat thighs of the plaster cherubs were as white as life; even the remote and secret windows let through an undimmed sun.

The King startled the silence. "Ho, thou leech," he cried, "where is my crown?"

"It is being repaired," said Sforelli, with a bow. "I have brought you back Sir Norman as I promised."

"You have been long absent, sir, though your King was in need of you. What have you achieved all these long days?"

"Sire," said Norman, "I have slain three dragons, a red, a yellow and a green: and all with horns upon their tails."

"But my dragon," said the King, impressively, "you have not slain. And to-night I must meet my Queen."

"Thy Queen, Sire?" said Sforelli, in evident surprise.

"Even so."

"That will be impossible unless the enchanter is slain."

"Then he must be slain at once," said the King, with resolution.

"Exactly, and that is why I have brought this good Knight. But your Majesty must drink a draught to protect you against enchantment."

"This last time I will obey you to obtain deliverance. I am sick of your potions. But beware; if he is not slain in time for the arrival of that paragon of the world, my Queen, I will—I will—" (the King frowned and hesitated to find words terrible enough) "—I will cut off all your toes and thread them in a necklace and hang them round your neck," he said in triumph.

"Bring the cup," said Sforelli to one of the guards, who immediately produced a rose-coloured liquid in a tumbler, which he handed to the King off a salver with some; ceremony. The King immediately drank it: the four men waited in silence as a happy smile began to play over the Royal features and he sank quietly asleep. The two guards then stripped him of his state robes and muffled him up in a great coat, and, followed by the doctor and Norman, took him out to the castle gate, where a closed carriage was waiting, and placed him inside. The doctor turned to Norman.

"I wonder what that was about his Queen? It's quite a new delusion and startled me."

"Some stir of Spring in him, perhaps," said Norman.

"Well, it's of little matter. We'll find out at the asylum. He will be better off there than here in many ways. It's cleaner, and he will have more fresh air. He is an interesting subject. Now, my unfortunate friend, as we arranged, you must wait in this place, I am afraid, till I return, which will not not be till near on dawn, for there is still much to do. As I said, I am afraid you will be lonely. I think you had better not show yourself out of this wing of the castle, and the guards cannot keep you company as they must stay at the gate. However, you will find a library, rather technical, perhaps, in my dissecting room. A couch has been prepared there, too, and I have not forgotten tobacco. No," continued the doctor, in response to a nervous look in Norman's face, "there is nothing there but books and implements," and the doctor with this assurance drove off with his capture.

On the way the lunatic began to recover from the effects of the drug. He sat in the carriage, now opening and now shutting an eye, and once mumbling some words about his Queen. Finally he went to sleep again. The doctor had but little parley at the diminutive asylum, a doll's house of a construction which he had built, and now managed. He ran it, indeed, at considerable profit, for the paying patients, offshoots of the noble families, considerably outnumbered such pauper inmates as he admitted free. He explained to the trusty guardian the deplorable delusions of the patient, and ordered certain comforts to be given him.

"You might also get him shaved," he added.

The guardian, who was a conspirator also, thoroughly understood the whole business. And there we can leave the doctor and return to Norman, who by no means enjoyed the situation. He did not find the books in the dissecting room of much interest. He was wandering in the throne-room, which looked more ghastly than ever, now the guards had extinguished the candles, in the flickering shadow of the lamp he carried, when he found several scraps of paper on the throne itself. They were covered with intricate designs and meaningless arabesques. There was a wing, there a face, there a foot, there an emblem—all incoherent and messed round with wild scratches. The bits of paper had so fearsome a fascination that it was almost a relief to Norman to go back to the dissecting room and sit down and try to read a treatise on skin diseases. But long before he had mastered the difficult subject Norman was on foot again, restless and troubled. The window was barred—Andrea had slept here sometimes. The night was close.

He sighed for the young strong arms that might have been round his neck. The conspiracy seemed already to be enclosing him in an impenetrable net. As immeasurable time wore on the fishy eyes of Andrea haunted him.

He would not sleep inside the bed, a sorry and comfortless pallet which might have been the madman's.

He lay down on it, dressed as he was, flinging off only his collar. Sleep would not come, save for fitful visions. Rising again, he saw his face pallid in the looking-glass by the light of the dingy candle, which flickered in a gorgeous stand of beaten copper. He blew the candle out hurriedly, then groped for matches, and lit it again, and flung himself once more on to the couch.

A fitful slumber was descending over him, prelude to sweet sleep, when he heard footsteps, with a tapping noise and the sound of voices. One voice was a man's: there were two other voices, of women. Norman leapt from the bed, alert, and listened hard.

"He won't hurt you, Drakina," said one voice. "He's kissed me many a time, and I don't know what he might not have done if Makzelo had not been there."

A confused giggle was all the reply Norman could hear.

"Where is he, Malsprita?" said another girl's voice.

"Hullo," said the voice of the man, apparently called Makzelo. "He seems to have gone away. The room's empty, that's strange."

"Perhaps he's gone to bed," said a girl.

"He can't have; he never goes to bed as early as this. We have played with him night after night. He loves it, doesn't he, Malsprita?"

"When I do it."

More giggles. Then the voice of Drakina was heard, saying she was frightened.

"Andrea!" cried Makzelo.

They all shouted; there was no reply.

"Let's go and look for him in the corridors. How strange! he was dreadfully excited about his Queen. He mustn't be disappointed."

"I'm frightened," said Drakina. "I don't want to be his Queen."

"You who wanted so to be in a real King's arms. What a little coward you are!"

"But the corridors are so dark. Is he very dreadful to look at, Malsprita?"

"He is not so ugly as you, club-foot! Nothing like."

There was a shuffling and tapping into the corridors.

Norman listened with wonder and disgust. Not quite realizing the meaning of the conversation, he had nevertheless understood enough to feel like a prisoner whose cell is full of rats. What nameless revels had these beings held? The nocturnal visits of these creatures were evidently unknown to Dr Sforelli. Here were three people who knew the Bang by sight: if this unexpected difficulty were not disposed of, the whole plot was ruined. At all events time must be gained: they must not be led to imagine the King already gone. What should he do? He had a second to deliberate while they went into the throne-room: but had made no plan when he heard them outside his door.

"Then he must be in his bedroom," said the man, and went over to open the door.

"Why, it's locked."

"Perhaps the doctor did it," said the club-foot girl.

"Let's burst it in!"

"I daren't disobey the doctor," said the man.

"That doctor's a devil. Why must he pretend the King's away?"

"For God's sake don't tell a soul."

"Andrea! Your Queen!"

"He must be sound asleep, or drugged," said a woman.

"Let's go and look in through the window," said the voice which Norman had by now identified as that of Malsprita.

"We might get a look at him, at all events. Always my luck; just the night I came."

"Well, we'll do that for you," said the man, pompously. He led them round outside. The club-foot girl continued moaning, "I was born crooked and ugly and crooked and ugly I shall die, and I might have been happy just once." And still complaining she passed out of earshot with the rest. Norman covered his head with a sheet, and crouched beneath the window, waiting. He heard the shuffle and tap coming along the gravel outside.

"Why, the bar's out," said the club-foot girl, and she poked her hideous head right through the window. It was a face neither of man nor woman, nor yet of utter evil, but rather of incarnate brutishness. It had no features but a mouth; it was a flat and fleshy face. In frenzy, Norman rose, emitting a falsetto shriek extremely piercing and horrible by which he frightened even himself, and dealt a terrific blow at the head with the great candlestick. By a surprisingly swift move the woman, if woman it was, avoided the bar, receiving the blow on her arm: she uttered a piercing shriek more ghastly still, and the three intruders rushed away into darkness. Losing for the first time in his life all his self-control, Norman kept on shouting and at the same time banged the candlestick against a tin basin, producing a desolating boom. Then he became quiet, relit the candle, and with a book in his hand, which he hardly read, now dozing, now awakening with a start if a leaf rustled or a mouse ran over the floor, stayed in his chair till he could endure it no longer and fled out into the open air.

The doctor on his return as he came with one of the guards through the entrance gate discovered Norman in the grey of dawn pacing the ruined garden and shivering with cold. He was much troubled when he heard the story. "I have been vilely negligent, and I ought to be ashamed of myself for forgetting the fellow," he said. "He was a sort of nurse to Andrea. I thought him too stupid and too frightened of me to do harm, and as he is not supposed to come here at night I had postponed dealing with him till to-day." And turning to the guard at his side, he bade him arrest the three persons concerned and keep them in close custody in the old keep. "Forget all that unpleasantness now, Sir," he continued, "and I beg of you to attend to more serious topics. The letters addressing an invitation to the notable people in the town to come and felicitate you on your cure are now ready and waiting for you to sign them. The said notables should be here this afternoon. You will receive them here in military uniform."

"And what shall I say to them? You have only told me the story of myself. How shall I greet them?"

"That, Sir, is for you to decide. We rely on you: you must rely on yourself."

CHAPTER XIII

RE-CORONATION

The world was made for Kings:
To him who works and working sings
Come joy and majesty and power
And steadfast love with royal wings!

The preliminary interview with the notables succeeded beyond expectation. No sign of doubt was displayed anywhere, and the happy suggestion was made that a re-coronation should take place a few days later, to coincide with the great Midsummer feast of San Adovani.

Vorza, who had rolled up to the meeting in his superb state coach, was extremely deferential. Norman detained him after for a private interview, ostentatiously dismissing even Sforelli.

"Alas!" said the King to him, "that so many years of helplessness have prevented me from a due appreciation of your untiring energies in the service of this realm. Be not afraid that I shall ever forget the old noble houses of Alsander. In you I know I can put my trust, and I will begin this auspicious day by honouring a tried and faithful servant of my family and the nation."

This said, Norman clapped his hands, and an attendant entered carrying on a cushion a collar set with pearls.

"Here are the insignia of the office of Lord Chamberlain," continued the King, "which I found in an old safe, tarnished with age and disuse. This I put round your neck and make you master of my household. I pray you now to arrange the procession. I have made Doctor Sforelli my secretary: consult with him if you will: he knows all the details. For the present," continued the King, confidentially, "I have need of Sforelli's services. For the present," he added in a low voice, with much insinuation.

Vorza left the presence somewhat mollified but still suspicious.

After this preliminary interview, following Sforelli's advice, Norman did not show himself abroad till the day of his re-coronation: and heard like a man imprisoned vague rumours of the stir outside. On the night of anticipation the young King—for so he shall be styled in future—slept little, and rising in the first grey of dawn he muffled himself in a coat and stepped out unseen upon a lofty balcony to look out upon the waiting crowd. Down there, in the cold misty break of a day that promised a relentless noontide sun, upturned faces were appealing stupidly for information to the granite castle walls. Weary men began to yawn and shuffle, and shifted the drowsy girls that slept upon their knees. Some were dozing on stools; others, seated on parapets, leant back uncomfortably against the rusty lamp-posts; others lay carelessly upon the pavement or on the pedestal of the statue of Kradenda.

"Truly," thought Norman, "they will be stiff men to rule, these people of Alsander: their heads are all the same shape."

The King was to step into his gilded coach in the company of Vorza and Sforelli: the guards had already cleared the road with unprecedented valour, while the amazing coachman perched himself expectantly upon the box as if he had been born for the task—and indeed the doctor had even found the family in which the tradition ran of driving this curious vehicle. Norman, dressed in military uniform, at the appointed hour left the throne-room, and with great solemnity was handed to his seat by the Lord Chamberlain, who then took his place in the Royal coach. They left the castle yard amid a roar of enthusiasm, and moved slowly down the main street of the town towards the Cathedral square. Such had ever been the processional route of the Kings of Alsander.

At last the carriage stopped at the grand porch of the Cathedral. There, after Norman had been robed in those same overpowering and sumptuous cloths of state that had been stripped from the unconscious Andrea, the ceremony of re-coronation took place. It proved to be an elaborate function, invented by an old-time Bishop with a passion for symbolism and an eye for scenic effect. It consisted of appropriate ritual minutiae, as, for instance, the re-anointing and replacing of the crown—which it would be tedious to describe in detail. But the closing scene of the service was superb. Norman raised himself from his knees, and turned towards the people, feeling his young body awkwardly stiff amid the heroic amplours of his purple robes, and in a few sentences promised to increase the glory of Alsander, making no reference to the mad years gone by. Idle to reproduce those simple sentences, without the animate vision of that clear voice, and the humorous, handsome face with its brilliant blue eyes; without knowing that most wonderful of Cathedrals, whose Byzantine mosaics seemed no less barbarous and splendid than the aristocracy, expectant beneath, whose jewels, the hoard of feudal treasure chests, glimmered and swayed dimly in the incense-laden choir.

And strange it was how when he made that speech the words of the boy rang true and sincere. In the glory of the ceremony he forgot the shabby and grotesque conspiracy: he became for the moment the King of Alsander: he meant the words he said.

The afternoon was ushered in by a long procession of girls and youths: the girls carrying little pots wherein grew wheat, cornflowers and poppies. They passed in Indian file before the Cathedral, and each fair girl that passed broke her pot against the door, in front of whose dinted panels soon grew up a little mountain of sherds, and earth, and fading flowers and corn. Then they passed down to the riverside, and the King followed them in state. There they found themselves face to face with the young men of Alsander, many of them in that gorgeous national costume of which Arnolfo was so fond, who had left them at the Cathedral door and had run round the bridge and were already facing them on the opposite bank. The youths threw off boots and socks, if they were wearing them, and coats, if they possessed them: neither did the girls fear to display their shapely feet: men and maidens entered the stream, the men valiantly, the maids demurely, and then, dipping their hands in the water, they began splashing each other vigorously across the river. When all were soaked with water many of the men swam over, seized a girl and ducked her in the stream: this was held to be a most solemn betrothal. For in the meantime the priests and the Cathedral choir had assembled on the bridge and young voices began to raise the old Latin hymn of the Consecration of the Waters, a hymn older than the Cathedral of Alsander itself, one of the oldest hymns in the world. Swiftly the tumult was stilled, and all knelt by the shore.

Raised on a platform behind the priests stood the tall King: he did not seem to share the joy of all the others, and while they knelt he shaded his eyes, but not for prayer, The first excitement of his adventure had passed: seeing now all around him in the clear and truthful sunlight this mock revel given in his honour and in honour of a lie, he felt a thief and a liar. There was no thrill of triumph in his heart for his achievement. His fellow conspirators had taken him into their farce as one might take a spectator from the stalls and dress him up for the role of King. In the farce nothing mattered—honour or right or manhood. Now here was reality to face him: he was a King, and an impostor. The amazing Arnolfo, whose fantasy and youth had given some poetry to the crude conspiracy, had deserted him. Women, and the fair woman he had seen in the light of morning—was it a thousand years ago?—were lost to him for ever. As amid the joyous sunshine of that first morning when he saw Alsander rise up above her meadows, when, afraid of the world's too deadly beauty, he had felt more lonely than ever in his life before, so now when he had achieved this marvellous thing, now that he ruled the ancient, fair and fabled city, he sank into utter desolation of the soul. And this time no golden girl would chase the black phantom of sorrow from his soul.

But as the great final major chords of the sumptuous old song rolled out above the river new courage came to him. He could not go back. He could not justify himself ever at any time at all. He realized that the plot had irrevocably succeeded: and that he was a prisoner for ever. Nevermore would he tramp the joyful mountains. To no new country could he direct his steps. To his own country and his own sweet village nevermore would he return. Love for women—the true, free love of a boy—henceforward he might never feel. Honest men he might never shake by the hand again. Severed from friends and the sweet companions of youth, he must thenceforth talk with wise or portentous or aged men.

Serious and sad, he looked at the beautiful city, shining above the shining river. He saw new visions, thought out new ideas, of a bitter and Spartan taste for a boy's sugared fancy. His soul and his conscience, his peace of mind, his friends, his love, his youth he flung down as an offering to the city. And like a man, he swore to work.

CHAPTER XIV

PRINCESS IANTHE

Là il vino, la luce, la nota che freme
Nei nervi, nel sangue, risveglian l'ardor.
Carducci.

Hardly in the history of Alsander, not when the first Kradenda laid the foundation-stone! of the Cathedral and all his warriors clashed their spears, nor yet in the silver age of Basilandron, when the youthful bands, clothed curiously, the women in gauze veils and the men in leopard skins, woke unhallowed revel beneath those sacred walls, when their trumpets blew for the bloodless battle, and the fifes played a prelude to amorous war, hardly in her days of victory or days of loveliness had the old castle square been so clamorous or splendid as on this night of the Royal feast. The sun had just set, and the afterglow was fading from the marble façade of the palace; the Queen of Night was on her throne; the bunting-covered trestle tables were prepared for a great feast which all Alsander was to attend. The wine stood ready in barrels: the huge Parisian carver, a master of his art, bared his bullock arms for the strife; servants staggered out from the castle kitchen with dishes; and already the people were beginning to assemble, for they heard the great horn of summoning blow clear and strong. The old men hobbled in on sticks, the middle-aged sniffed the viands, the young men came joyously along with laughter and the lasses. Seven thousand voices cried "Amen" to the Archbishop's meandering Latin grace: and amid an uproar of delight the Bang himself lit the vast bonfire prepared in the midst, the immemorial bonfire of the feast day, which was to be now a welcome compensation for the vanished light and warmth of the sun.

For the day was to end, as it had begun, with the full glory of mediaeval pageant, and by unbroken tradition each new-crowned King had to give a feast to his townfolk to celebrate his coronation. But this was a specially noble and glorious ceremony—it was more than a coronation: it was a re-coronation—and Alsander expected that amends would be made for the inglorious day when, amid a winter rain, a thin and draggled concourse of spectators watched the closed carriage which they were told contained a King that was no King and a man that was no man. And now, behold, they had a King indeed, who looked strangely unlike a convalescent madman—a King as young and beautiful and strong as a woman's heart could wish to break for—a King of perfect utterance and fine presence whom any loyal gentleman would be proud to serve. A King, moreover, who had already come and lived among the humblest of his people like a simple stranger. What more could Alsander desire?

Happy and blest was the table which enjoyed the company of one of those who had known the King during his stay at the Widow Prasko's. Willing enough were they all to talk, little Pedro, Father Algio, the old Widow Prasko herself, and the rest of them, as fast as they could for eating and drinking the choicer morsels and wines with which they were specially plied by their admiring boon companions. It was wonderful how many people had known the King intimately during those few weeks—with how many he had held long and confidential conversation about the politics of Alsander. It was curious how not one of them had been deceived an instant by his story of being an Englishman. Whoever heard of a foreigner who spoke Alsandrian! Of course, he pretended to speak it badly: how wise and clever and beautiful he was! They had heard to-day how he could speak the language—and so forth, and so forth.

Those who had really known the King were full, too, of the brightest fancies. What honours and rewards would be showered on them for the little services they had rendered? One poor, penniless fellow, who had once shown Norman the way, put on the most ridiculous airs after a few glasses of strong red wine. He was already enjoying the fruits of a fine pension, and wandering through the palace courts in cloth of gold.

Only Peronella sat in absolute silence by her mother's side. Not a word would she answer to any question, despite the harsh rebukes of her expansive parent. She sat and drank rather much and ate almost nothing. All those around her affected to understand her mood and ceased to trouble her with questions. It was plain the King had broken her heart. Well, was it not the high tradition of Royalty to break the hearts of humble women? thought the men of Alsander. Could the King have chosen a lovelier girl? Doubtless the King would see her again and not desert her quite absolutely for ever. The flower-like Peronella was made to be a Royal Mistress. The men of Alsander praised her beauty, her reticence and her air of sorrow, which they conceived to be if not genuine at least most nobly affected, while the women of Alsander were consumed with the most passionate jealousy and envy of the poor girl. But what of Peronella?

Peronella was a girl with a simple soul, but the simplest of souls is, after all, according to the idealists, a more wondrous and complex thing than the mechanism of the latest Dreadnought. A soul, being alive, grows and changes. Peronella had to-day discovered that she loved Norman with all the love her soul could give—and only simple folk like her can give all their souls to love. She had no preoccupation with the world save to find therein; a man to love, and she had found Norman. And now he was gone from her—taken far away. She knew her lover had abandoned her for ever!

She had become a woman. It was not this sudden Royalty that made her love the boy who so few weeks ago had come to her singing over the mountain height. It was the shock of it all—and the separation. For others might believe this tale. Others—and they became many as the wine flowed round—might whisper dark whispers, and swear that it was incredible that this bright northern-faced boy should be a Kradenda, and hint of a cunning and tremendous plot. But she alone of all the uninitiated folk of Alsander knew with the sure and instinctive knowledge of a woman for an absolute certainty that the re-coronation was a farce and that Norman was no more King of Alsander than she was Queen. And the sorrow on her face was but the genuine reflection of the agony of her soul, but her agony was not for her country's misfortune but for a lover lost.

But meanwhile the feast was progressing, and a clamour arose that made one think more of Flanders and the north and the gross banquets of Jordaens than of southern frugality and moderation.

The King, in the dark green uniform of an Alsandrian Colonel, with Vorza, Sforelli, the nobles, their ladies, our old friend the British Consul (in a cocked hat) and his colleagues, each of whom hoped shortly to acquire the title of Minister to so energetic a Court, were seated, together with a few very distinguished correspondents of great newspapers, who had been invited to the Royal board by special request, at a long table under the open gates, beneath the door of the castle. Arnolfo had not reappeared. The general conversation was lively and elegant: but Norman—whose ostensible knowledge of the world had to be confined to the castle walls, a few books, a few weeks in Alsander, and a year in a "home" in England, hardly dared open his mouth. This need of caution, this forced lying masquerade, and a longing not only for Peronella, but also for the companionship of the strange young man who alone seemed to have the power of turning life into a furious and careless dream made him so gloomy that Vorza was very frightened lest in some uncanny outbreak of revived mania the King should hurl his plate at the head of his newly-appointed Lord Chamberlain. Nevertheless, this sullen reserve which the King displayed suited the part he had to play (as an interesting example of scientific progress) to perfection. When, however, at times he woke up from his pensive and melancholy meditations, he was possessed with a sort of odd! feeling that he must give the newspaper gentlemen some copy, and would talk gravely of the careful reforms he would make in; the drainage of the city, the paving of the streets and the training of the militia, or sigh for his wasted youth with intense pathos, saying, too, how glad he would be when these formalities were over and he could tour round his dominions, "which are, despite a few weeks' residence in the city itself, as strange to me, sir," he said, addressing the special correspondent of the Daily Mail, "as they are to you." Towards the end of the meal, he was seized by an idea which comforted him, and became suddenly so gay that the doctor trembled for his dignity and, pretending to be concerned for his still precarious health, advised him in an audible whisper not to tire himself by too much lively conversation.

After the enormous repast was at length ended, the guests scattered for a digestive interval preliminary to the splendid dance which was to end the day. The doctor regaled some ecstatic Ulmreich medicine men with tales, all in the strictest confidence, of the surprising operations that had been performed on the King, while the King walked round with Vorza, asking the delighted Duke many questions about the government and still more about the evening's ceremonial.

"Of course I rely on you, my Lord Chamberlain," he explained, "for all ceremonial details. Though, alas! you have no experience in your duties, you have, I feel sure, that exquisite tact which as the great Court historian Brasaldo says, is the exclusive birthright of ancient and honourable families."

Vorza bowed.

"Now, I believe there is to be a dance to-night as soon as the tables have been removed."

"The musicians should be here in an hour's time, your Majesty."

"They will be good musicians, I hope."

"I believe so, Sire. They are world renowned."

"Now, my Lord, when the last King was crowned, as I read once in Brasaldo's history—one of the very few books I have read all through...."

Vorza bowed again, in deference, perhaps, to such heroic perseverance.

"The last King—my father, I mean, whom I remember but faintly, for I was such a little boy when the trouble came—danced, I believe, in accordance with traditional custom with several of the fairest maidens of the town."

Vorza was quite reassured by this token of the Royal sanity, and bowed again.

"Now, of course, for me—all thoughts of woman's loveliness have no charm: I am tool inexperienced, alas! What a youth I have had!—I have had none, rather. But since the ceremony is old and picturesque I should like to; revive it."

"But, Sire, between me and your Majesty, you have not had time to learn to dance."

This was unexpected, but Norman rose to the occasion.

"You know little of England and modern curative establishments," he said. "The regime of the whip and straight waistcoat is over, thank God, or you would not have the pleasure of my company to-night. Three days' sojourn is not quite enough for that wonderful country, my lord."

Vorza smiled, but sinister thoughts passed through his heart.

"It must have been a marvellous place indeed, Sire, this home to which the gooch luck of Alsander sent you. But will you never tell the secret of its locality? For it would be only right, between me and your Majesty, to honour the wise director with a national tribute."

"It is not his desire," said Norman, briefly. "But with regard to this dance to-night, I want to know my people. I propose that the dance should be promiscuous, and I will join it myself."

"That is quite in accordance with the best traditions of Alsander, your Majesty," said Vorza, and he promised to make the announcement in due form.

Vorza left him, and for a moment he stood alone and looked round on the scene of revel, and at that moment the uproar of gross feeders and drinkers seemed to pause a second, drowned in the vast fullness of the jasmine night. Then the musicians began from their bower among the shadowy plane trees—glorious musicians, and so glorious a music that not a man would dare to dance to it, for all that the orders were that none should wait for the Kong. All listened immobile: only the Japanese lights and those further lights the stars dared to start off dancing to such a tune. All the new power and subtlety of modern music seemed to have blended with the grand traditions of olden days to make this lovely melody: yet the melody was a waltz—a waltz-tune that the simplest could understand and that set the body dancing. Another instant and the spell broke: the music became human and the whole square which the carpenters had turned into a vast dancing floor, was alive with couples, and seemed itself to turn.

And the great sense of the unreality of the world again took possession of Norman. It seemed to him that he was a King indeed but a true King, the King in a fairy story, and might do what he will. If he was to play this splendid part, he would not play as a modern King—a tired, frock-coated slave of wearisome Ministers. He would be a King of Yvetot, of Atlantis, of the Indian Isles. He would; dance with Peronella—was it not the old! custom that he should dance with the fairest of his subjects? Would he not be the more beloved for his boldness? If he were not, what matter? The girl should be his mistress that night; to his great golden room he would lead her, and for one night he would celebrate Aphrodite. Was it not for this that she had been sent by destiny to meet him—swinging her pails beside the spring on that immortal morning? Was it not for this one night that he had played the supremest farce that ever a man played?

He started to find her, motioning away those that would accompany him. He soon caught sight of her, a little way off seated alone on a bench, as though she awaited him, and looking towards him with her eyes shining in the light of the lamp. His heart beat, and he trembled as he had never done through all his play-acting. He knew still that to steal a maiden's honour was a greater enterprise than to ravish a throne. He knew he had but one step further to take toward the girl, who sat there trembling with love to receive him. His foot was light on the ground to take that step—for what to a King is all the world?

Yet at that moment a hand was laid on his arm to arrest him. He looked round, and saw Arnolfo. The boy was clothed as ever in Alsandrian dress but of a darker hue: he was cloaked, and the silver buckles of his belt gleamed beneath the rich and sombre mantle. In this raiment, at such an hour, he looked paler than the moon, and strangely moved, yet resolute as death.

Norman knew why Arnolfo had laid the hand on his arm: he saw the will and determination on the boy's face: he knew that his scheme was known, and that it was to be frustrated. He swung round on his heel. "Leave me!" he said with passion, but his voice was not that of a King who rules the world, but of an angry boy.

"Did I not tell you to keep from women, my King," pursued Arnolfo. "Surely I am only just in time."

"It is too late! Your dramatic interventions are useless. I go where I please. You should not have left me in the lurch all these days if you wished to remain my mentor. I am master now. Leave me: we are not unobserved: you are making me ridiculous before my subjects."

"My Bang, I implore you as a friend, come away with me," said Arnolfo in a voice strangely passionate.

"A friend are you? You have made a fool of me for ever. I have got to play-act all my life. You have stolen from me my love, my liberty and my youth. You have left me alone to carry through the most perilous portion of this mad enterprise, and now, when I want to rescue a few moments of joy from the ruin of my life, you say, 'Friend! Friend!' Let me go, I tell you! Let me enjoy the glory of existence for one hour before you shut me in your dismal prison of lies for ever!"

And Norman pointed to the grim, dark, towering walls of the palace of Kradenda.

But Arnolfo, with that magic power that never failed to influence Norman—to influence him so deeply that it seemed able at times to sap his very manhood and honour—for, after all, he had suffered the utmost degradation at this boy's command—Arnolfo had already drawn Norman away and Norman was following him, why, he knew not, towards the palace.

"Come, Norman," said Arnolfo, in that low and honeyed voice of his, "a friend is better than a lover, as love is better than lust."

"For Kings!" exclaimed Norman, but whether as a question or in bitter acquiescence was not certain from the sound of his voice.

"O come with me a minute," said Arnolfo, pretending still to plead and drawing Norman further and further at each step from Briseis. "All your happiness may depend on that. Will you ruin yourself and Alsander for a pretty face? Are you going to play tyrant and drag her from the arms of her lover?"

"Damnation on duty and on you and all this farce!" replied the King, muttering low as he turned for a last look at the girl who, still visible, was now standing with bowed head, her arm around a young sapling—and still alone. "Were it not for your fool's mummery I might have had that girl in my arms. Look at her: is she not beautiful enough for you, my artist? Are not these lips red enough for the Sultan of the Indies? Where is the lover from whose arms I should drag her? Leave me, Arnolfo. Must I forget my youth."

"Give me one half-hour—alone—in the palace. After that, you shall be free of my interference for ever and return to your love If you so desire. I swear it. But come now. There is ... danger. Ah, Norman, can you not read sincerity in the eyes?"

Involuntarily Norman looked at the boy and saw in his eyes a light so strange that he was troubled. The charm of Arnolfo had already compelled him: but now his very passion surrendered to it. Without more complaint, he broke with him through the crowd, which opened to let him pass.

None ventured to attend them. The guards seemed to Norman to show as much deference in their salutes to Arnolfo as to himself. They went alone together to a little room in the tower, where a lamp was hanging—simply to aid in the general illumination, for the room was empty and unfurnished.

"Well," said Norman turning on his friend with some fierceness, "tell me your story."

The boy flushed a little. "There is no story," he said.

"But you said there was danger in what I intended to do. Not that I mind, but tell me what you meant."

"You neither were nor are in any danger."

"Then why, in God's name," cried Norman "did you bring me Here?"

Arnolfo put a finger to his lips and leant over the stone window-sill to gaze at the crowded square. "You ask why I brought you here, King of Alsander," he whispered toi Norman, who stood over him. "Oh, can you not yourself discover why? Can you draw no inspirations from the world around you? Will nothing but brutal speech make you understand? Cannot music suggest to you the truth, or the rustle of leaves, or the murmur of men down there that makes audible the silence of the stars? Is there no subtler essence in nature or your own soul ready to vibrate? Has not the Universe a dumb but smiling mouth to say why I brought you here?"

"Heavens, what weird nonsense you are talking," said Norman, catching the boy's arm, "Can you not speak straight? Or what new web of perplexity are you weaving for my destruction?"

"Leave me," said the boy with a gasp, as though Norman's clutch on his arm had hurt him. "Leave me: I will go: you shall never see me again. Keep your peasant girl, Norman Price: who shall blame you? Real kings have fared far worse."

"I want to know what you meant about the silence," said Norman looking curiously into his friend's pale face and expressive eyes. "And what my peasant girl has got to do with you."

"How can you stand almost touching me!" cried Arnolfo, leaping up from the window and facing Norman with a sort of indignation. "How can you put your hand on my arm and still not know and still be such a fool! And they talk of instinct! I am ashamed at my failure. Ah, how did I dare bring you here?"

And turning again to the window Arnolfo buried his face in his hands and wept.

"Why, you strange creature, what have you got to weep for?" cried Norman in dismay. "You trouble me with your strange ways to-night. I swear if you are unhappy I will do my best to comfort you; but do speak straight out, and do above all be a man."

The boy looked up, and through his tears he smiled, and then through his tears he laughed. And then he simply laughed very prettily and held out his right hand.

"Look at my hand a minute," he said.

Norman took the proffered hand and examined it with great embarrassment and wonder. "It is a very small hand," he said; "but I don't see what is the matter with it."

Then at last suspicion flashed across his mind. "Ah, you don't mean that!" he cried, suddenly dropping the hand and starting back.

"Good God," laughed Arnolfo rather wildly. "I can't think of any more hints to give you, barbarian! Must I strip to the waist?"

Norman gasped. "If you really are a woman, Arnolfo," he exclaimed, "I would much prefer that you did."

Then he stood motionless before her and for a time the two faced each other without a word, the King with his hand on the hilt of his sword, and the woman clasping across her body the great mantle, as though to preserve even at this hour, the virginity of her disguise.

"I am the Princess Ianthe," she said at last, with a dignity which the travesty could not obscure.

"You are a very beautiful woman," rejoined Norman, bending to kiss her hand. Then, looking at her with a rather inscrutable smile which strangely aged his youthful face, he added: "but I bitterly regret the loss of Arnolfo."

The Princess hung her head a little and seemed almost the boy again. "Is that all you have to say?" she murmured, "and yet there is nothing I would rather you had said than that."

"It was for Arnolfo I adventured on this enterprise," pursued the King gravely, "for his friendship I ruined my life to become a mummer and a thief. And now the pantomime continues—and there is no Arnolfo."

"But you have Ianthe's friendship," cried the Princess, "as you had Arnolfo's."

He shook his head. "Friendship with a woman is not a sport for kings."

"But such a friendship as ours," she rejoined, "cannot be broken by an epigram."

"It is broken," affirmed the King. "The days of friendship are irrevocably over. And I have no reason to think, Princess, although you singled me out to rule your country, and although I, when I found you a woman, was stirred with something that was not only wonder, that the halcyon days are near. And yet—I am speaking to you straight, Princess, in the English way—if you do not think we shall become more than friends I shall leave you and Alsander to-night for ever, and see what fresh adventures await me in the teeming world. Maybe some other country will greet me as its King and a princess only a little less beautiful than you, in a realm a little more fabulous than Alsander, will offer me her heart and hand. But I will simply laugh and go back home to England. One day of kingship has been enough for me."

"And is that all you have to say to a woman who has given you a Crown and to a people who are awaiting their King? Have you no fire, no pride?"

"I have a sense of honour," replied the King gravely. "For listen to me. You have given me a crown of gold, and it is a crown of thorns. You have made me a mock King. I am already weary, unutterably weary. What care I for Alsander? Is not a hedgerow in my native land lovelier than all its cypress trees? What care I for ruling—save to be the master of a straight young woman, and lord of a country farm? On one condition only will I consent to endure this foolery one more day, and that is on condition that you—the heiress of Alsander—become rightfully my Queen, for all that I am an English grocer boy. I am no fool, Princess, and I may dare to hope that you will accept this condition, for I think some such project has been in your mind all the time, through all this queer history. But I have a second condition, which is harder, and that condition is this: that if you love me, I will be your King. If you love me with all your heart and soul, as I love you, and only in that case, then we will rule our land together. And if not, Ianthe, bid farewell to me to-night—for you will never see me again. The masquerade is over: speak truth to me at last."

"You are right!" said the Princess. "Must we talk like fanciful children and waste words, we on whom depends the fate of thousands, we the rulers of Alsander! You have made your conditions: I accept the first. I will be your Queen, in name and in deed, if you will. The Princess Ianthe, O King of Alsander, has also a sense of honour. I have made you a false King—I alone can make you a true King, the consort of the legitimate Princess of Alsander. I offer to be your Queen."

"But my second condition—your love, Princess Ianthe?"

"What do you mean by love? Is it my body you mean by my love? I owe it to you if you desire it. It shall be yours—I have promised to be your Queen. Or is it that, together with my true and loyal friendship you desire? That also shall be yours, though you have rejected it, for all my life long."

"I want your love, your true love, your deep love, the love of all your soul," said the King in a low voice, gazing into her brown eyes.

"Ah! that is not mine to command."

"Will it never be mine to command, Ianthe? Speak truth. If it will never be mine, I will not be King of Alsander."

"You are almost wooing me," exclaimed the Princess, laughing a little nervously, "and I rather wish I were dressed for the part. But is it not rather fantastic to claim my love without offering your own? And is it not rather insolent," she added abruptly, as though a flash of memory had caused a flash of rage, "for a man who has given his heart to a peasant girl to demand the love of a Princess?"

"You are insincere in your reproaches," replied the King. "You know from the very sound of my words that I have forgotten all the women of the world but you. You know I stand on the threshold of Love's house: but how do I know if you will ever join me, to enter side by side?"

Ianthe laid her hands lightly on the King's shoulder. "You will not win me before you woo, ungallant heart!" said she. "But if the day comes when you decide that I am worthy of your attentions, remember that my love, like that of fairy Princesses of China or of Ind, must be won by high achievement. It may be that I could, like a woman without shame, cry out this very hour, 'I love you,' were it not that my heart is lost already, pledged to a passion which surpasses all love I can feel for man. My body's love I will gladly give to whoever, like you, is beautiful and young, my friendship to whoever, like you, is gentle and wise, but my soul's love is my love for the Holy City of Alsander. There is not a court or a garden, not a stone of the cobbles of Alsander over which I would not slaughter the lover of my body or the friend who kept my thoughts if that would keep these holy streets from pollution and slavery. I love this country as no one has ever loved it before, save he who made it, my forefather, the great Kradenda. Its air is to me a more pellucid air, its rocks more ancient, its sea more blue, its flowers more fragrant than other airs and rocks and seas and flowers. And if a man would desire to have part of this deep love—and even with a part of it to be loved as no hero was ever loved in days of old by the great-bosomed women of the Greeks, then that man must become part of Alsander. He must fight, work, strive, for the glory of the kingdom. He would have his reward: for I am not a capricious woman but one whose heart is true, girl as I am.

"But do not answer me now: the minutes are flying on: your subjects will miss you: we must go out again into the square. Quick! I hear no more the dancers laughing and the splendid music has ceased sighing among the stars; they are waiting for their King to join them. Listen! The Cathedral bells of Alsander are tolling the midnight hour."

CHAPTER XV

PERONELLA AND THE PRIEST

Creep, and let no more be said.
Matthew Arnold.

The prolonged absence of the King having given rise to no small anxiety, there was universal relief at his reappearance, and he was welcomed with uproarious cheers as he stepped out of the palace gates, preceded by the Royal torchbearers. The King regretted to those of his notable guests whom he chanced to meet that affairs of State should have demanded his attention even on so holiday an evening. Sforelli also, by the Royal command, told Vorza to let it be known quietly that the King's health would not permit of his dancing that evening. To counteract the disappointment of this announcement, the King went round, with "Arnolfo" in attendance, among his subjects, conversing kindly with them and especially with those who were already his acquaintance. And seeing Peronella clinging to her mother, the widow, he did not hesitate, but went up to the couple, and after thanking the old lady for the excellent care she had taken of her Englishman, he praised her cooking, especially of beans and potatoes, and the softness of her linen, and the charm of her daughter. He then asked them both to come and pay him a visit in the course of the week. But not by a look, a sign, or a glance did he show to Peronella that he still loved or even that he still wanted her, In her new wisdom, born of bitterness of heart, the girl understood that her day was over, and inwardly she cursed Norman, and the mysterious young man at his side, who had so often taken him away from her, and the day that she was born.

"Ah, Norman," said Ianthe, as they left the group, in her low and gentle tones, "I see you are playing the game bravely. But you must play it as if you loved it, for it is a game for the glory of Alsander—if you do not love Alsander you cannot love its Queen; and if you do love Alsander, then, perhaps—but, hush! There is Vorza, dodging us round the statue."

The King beckoned to Vorza, who had just appeared from behind the pedestal of the statue of Kradenda, and was walking apparently in meditation. The Duke bowed. "Your Majesty," he said.

The King felt that an explanation of his apparently intimate converse with young Arnolfo was needed.

"Count Vorza," he said, pleasantly, "this young man, for all that he is the most charming of young men and a friend of yours and mine, is importunate. It is only my coronation day—my first evening of reign—and he is already trying to interest me in affairs of State."

"He is misguided but young," said Vorza, trying to catch the King's amiable tone of banter.

"He is misguided and young," echoed the King. "I have also noted in him a certain flightiness, eccentricity and weakness of purpose. But it seems he also has ambition."

"Ambition!" said Vorza, genuinely startled. "I have known him as the gayest and most delightful young man in Alsander, but he is surely not interested in affairs of State!"

"We have been deceived, Count Vorza. He is an enthusiast. He hopes to reform us all. He desires a post in the government."

"Surely he would be out of his element in serious affairs—if your Majesty and the gracious subject of our conversation will pardon my saying so!"

"I do not know, Vorza; I do not know. We need enthusiasts, we need youth. His father, however mistaken in his views, is an able man, and the ability may be inherited. I should like to give him a place in the government—but what place? I ask your advice, my Lord Chamberlain."

"I have no hesitation in giving it, your Majesty. My poor experience is always at your service and the service of the country. If any government post be given to this young man, it must be the Ministry of Fine Arts—a post which I am sure he would fill with distinction."

"I am entirely of your opinion, Count Vorza. The appointment shall be gazetted to-morrow."

Upon which the Count withdrew, meditative but not gloomy. If such young fools were to be the King's favourites, there would be ample opportunity for him to continue wielding the supreme power in Alsander. For a moment he forgot his suspicions as he dreamt the dreams of a man whose ambition age has sharpened instead of dulled.

But late that night when guests and populace (as it had been arranged for the sake of the King's supposed weak health) had dispersed, Vorza, as he jogged home in his carriage, and looked back on the events of the day, was again seized with the conviction that both he and Alsander had been the victims of a childish, simple and audacious hoax. He raged inwardly. Suppose it were found out by some outsider, and he—he, the wise Vorza—were shown to have been miserably fooled by an English jester and a Jew doctor? Was young Arnolfo a plotter, too—had he secret instructions from his old scoundrel of a father? Either, Vorza determined, the hoax must remain unexposed or he must expose it. Pacing the quiet flags of his great hall he passed the hours till morning.

Meanwhile the King had formally dismissed his guests, none of whom were staying in the Castle, which, despite the efforts of plumbers, scullions, chambermaids and upholsterers, could only just accommodate with decency the King himself. As he entered the great gate the guard fell back, and he suddenly discovered with a queer thrill that the boy-princess had appeared from nowhere in particular and that they were walking together in the palace garden, the little ruined garden of King Basilandron, which at night, now that the little summer-houses and temples had all their graceful lines traced out with rows of Fairy lamps, had an air not of decay but rather of mystery and sweetness, so tangled were its bowers, so heavy hung the scent of roses in the air. Norman trembled, feeling the enchantment of the moonlight and all the fear that comes with the birth of passion; but he listened in silence to the silvery accents of the Princess as she told her tale.

It seems the admirable old Count Arnolfo was, as the Princess had described him to Norman when she pretended to be his son, sent to Alsander on a patriotic mission. The real son existed, but had been in America for many years; the real father was, as the Princess had depicted him, an ardent patriot, a man, however, of liberal views. He let the Princess run fairly wild—shocking a good deal the other little Royal households with whom they came into contact and giving rise thereby to the legends of her wildness that had reached even Alsander. But, naturally enough, even his liberal and easy mind would not have contemplated the possibility of his charge roaming Alsander in boy's attire. What old Count Arnolfo had done, however, was to sanction the Princess to make a journey incognito (not, indeed, that such a very unimportant and impoverished Princess would have been much disturbed by adventurers) with her trusty governess, Miss Johnson. Old Arnolfo was getting too old to wander far from home, but he felt all the same that the Princess ought to have a course of good, healthy eye-opening travel in the English fashion.

They were to go anywhere they liked except—and the old man warned them like Bluebeard admonishing his wives—except into the kingdom of Alsander. And of course, like Blue-beard's wife, Ianthe was fired with a resolve to go. But she did not know how to carry out the resolve, though she often thought of simply going and leaving Miss Johnson to her fate. It was the thought of getting poor Miss Johnson into trouble that prevented her from carrying out this plan rather than any fear of the difficulties of the enterprise. So the Princess kept quiet and toured the helpless Miss Johnson round, and wrote at regular intervals letters to her guardian full of admirable descriptions of the places and monuments visited, culled from Baedeker's well-known hand-books. In the monotony of luxurious travel she all but forgot Alsander.

But one night (and as she began to say one night, Norman, who had cared little to hear the long story, was caught to attention by the music of her words)—one night in London she leant out of her window and watched the Thames shining in the light of the moon. All the dark chimneys across the water were dancing in the moonlight like heavenly towers: and she almost loved the city that till then had seemed so hateful and so dark that she could not understand why men suffered to dwell therein. Then down the embankment came a man singing—but what was he singing? Not the latest infamy of the halls, nor yet a hearty British ballad—but the Song of the Black Swans of the Kradenda which every Alsandrian knows and loves. The singer passed beneath her window: she cried out, "Who goes there singing Alsandrian in the City of London?" Miss Johnson was shocked. The singer replied in English, "Who speaks to me in Alsandrian in a voice that is like a song?" Looking more closely, the Princess saw the singer to be a venerable and beautiful old man.

"I am an Alsandrian: speak English no more," she replied to his question.

"Ah! but I must speak English," said the stranger.

"But why?"

"Because I am an Englishman, fair lady of Alsander," replied the poet, for it was he, as Norman had already guessed.

A little disappointed, as she confessed, the Princess told how, nevertheless, she called the poet to come in and see her, and to a scandalized protest from Miss Johnson merely rejoined that if he might not come in through the door he should enter through the window.

It was the poet, then, who arranged the secret visit of Ianthe to Alsander. It was he who suggested her disguise, he who made friends for her in Alsander who could be trusted with the great secret, he who managed Miss Johnson. This latter superhuman task he managed heaven knows how. But I think the little old lady was a romantic and would have come, too, had it not been necessary for her to continue the tour and post from various illustrious towns the charming letters which the Princess with the poet's aid (to lighten the touch of Baedeker) composed beforehand ready for the post. "And so ends my tale," concluded the Princess. "Three days ago Sforelli, at my request, informed my guardian of all the amazing truth: and he (stern old man!) without one comment, has ordered me back. I must obey. I leave to-night. Here ends the masquerade!"

"Poor masquerade!" cried Norman. "Is it here the curtain falls? Whatever be the strong and radiant drama of our lives on which it shall rise again, I regret the masquerade!"

Their footsteps ceased upon the garden path. The moonlight flung their stilly shadows to the tattered roses. On the pediment of Love's plaster Temple one fairy light still palely glimmered in the vast white splendour of chaste Artemis. A nightingale trilled once, then fell a-dreaming. And through the boy's learned soul passed murmurs of ages far estranged, which yet blended together and took on a nature of their own—a clear dim note of the Athenian lyre, hinting beneath all artificial chords the melody of the earth and of truth, a gavotte by Lully or Rameau, a laugh of Heine, or songs they sang at the Cremorne Gardens, twenty years ago. He felt the moonlit sky, the ruined bowers, the Temple and the roses dwindle and shapen into the scenery of a stage—as though the girl in travesty before him had made a mockery of all the linked worlds. Then suddenly he knew.

"Columbine," he said, "you will not leave me thus?"

She stepped away from him lightly, arms akimbo.

"And what are you to me, Pierrot?" she cried; "or Columbine to you?"

"To me," he answered, "you are the colour of the soul of the marble statues, and the shape of the movement of the gliding moon."

"Like her," she laughed, "I shine falsely and I shine pale. Like her, to you I am only a shape that is no shape and a colour that is no colour."

"I will chase you from shape to shape," replied the young King. "I will pursue you from hue to hue; though you change to a slim gazelle or silver fish or a little seed of corn. And when I have conquered you at last, and held you, and driven you to your true and pristine form, then victorious, as now vanquished, will I swear eternal passion at your feet."

And he knelt on one knee before her.

"Why, Pierrot!" she whispered, "you said you would not love me yet!"

"But that," he replied, "was three hours ago."

"Pursue me no more, Pierrot," she warned him. "The moon has tricked your eye: the scents of the garden have deceived your heart. Am I not still Arnolfo? am I not still a boy?"

"Columbine," he replied, "I am pleading for love. Answer me now, tell me my doom, torment me no longer, for I hear approaching the fiery wheels of your departure."

"Oh, what a thirst for words you have," sighed she. "Stay there on your knees in silence, impatient, importunate Pierrot, and wait till I choose to answer."

"They have come to take you away!" he cried. "Your dragon is roaring at the gate. Your answer, Columbine!"

"Oh, stay there kneeling as I bid you," she cried, "and forget your thirst for words. Was it your mother, boy, who gave you eyes that colour in the night? Stay there and do not speak or raise your glance till you hear my dragon rolling me away—and let me give you, in my own fashion, the silent answer of my farewell."

She spake, and the very dragon ceased to roar, as though even his steely heart recognized the bell-like voice of his mistress, commanding silence throughout the world. Haunted with expectation Norman bowed his eyes: soon he felt her presence bending over him its wings. Softly her arm stole across his shoulder, and suddenly, to his great wonder, fell over his cheek a wave of the soft and fragrant hair he had never seen; and on his lips she answered him.

Too soon she was gone: but he obeyed her to the end; ecstasy which had snatched his spirit out into the realms of fire, had left his body frozen like ice and statues and the moon. He listened immobile to her step fading down the garden: he heard the rumour of her departure. Then he rose and like a man whom life has forgotten, he walked slowly back to his royal home.

But as for Peronella, she, poor girl, had made her way home early enough, clinging to her mother, not heeding the pity, envy, laughter or ridicule of the revellers, dozens of whom pointed to her to make their comment—so famous was she now. On her arrival she paid no attention to her mother's attempts to reassure her (which consisted in the reflection that no harm had been done, and the assertion that the King would provide her with a magnificent dowry), but rushing to her room, as ten thousand million disappointed maids have done before, she flung herself on the bed and burst into tears. Then she opened her box and took out a letter. A little slip may ruin a great cause, and the conspirators, who had thought to make all their plans so neatly and completely, had forgotten about letters. And this was a letter, with a British postmark and addressed to Norman Price.

"All Alsander may be deceived," cried Peronella to herself. "But I'll be even with the liar." Peronella, after a moment's hesitation, opened the letter with a little knife, cunningly, so that it could be sealed again. It was, of course, in English, so she could not understand it. She put it under her pillow with a peasant's caution, and cried herself to sleep.

The next morning she found Father Algio—whom she sought—at the confessional.

"You do well to come to me," said the priest, kindly. "You have been away too long."

"Ah! father," said Peronella, with a not quite honest sigh.

"The ways of Princes are not our ways, Peronella, and hard is the lot of the women whose path they cross."

"Princes?" said Peronella. "Do you believe that tale? A Prince—that Englishman who said he loved me?"

"What do you mean, my daughter? Which tale?"

"Do you believe that that Englishman who came to stay with us was our King Andrea?"

"But who ever doubted it, girl?" rejoined the old priest, pretending greater astonishment than he felt, for, after all, similar questions had been in the hearts of many. "In that he came to Alsander in secret for a few days before his accession we all count it for great wisdom on his part. You must be mad, girl, to talk such treason. Could all our rulers be lying to us?"

"Well, read this letter," said Peronella. "I cannot, for it is in English. It is addressed to him under the name he had when he was with me. It arrived after he left."

The worthy priest, who had been expecting a sad confession of deviation from the straight path of virtue, was more shocked than he would have been at any weakness of the flesh, at this manifestation of coldness, pettiness and deceit. (He need not be therefore accused of having hoped for a romantic tale. His long experience told him that small sins were sometimes worse than great ones.)

"Give me the letter," he said. Taking it, he addressed the girl severely. "You have committed many sins," he said. "You have sinned in stupidly doubting your lawful King; in thinking yourself cleverer than all the rest of Alsander; in taking a letter, which was not yours; in opening that letter and in attempting to disclose its contents to another. I shall reseal the letter and send it instantly to the palace: nor will I betray my King by giving a single glance at the contents. I am most displeased with you, my daughter."

"You will think differently of me when you have read the letter," sneered Peronella, rising and departing abruptly down the aisle with a confident and cynical laugh—a laugh sad years older than her laughter of a week ago.

The old priest looked after her with melancholy eyes, then let his glance fall on the letter. He then read it.

Father Algio was a strictly virtuous and honourable old man. He must, therefore, have had good reason for acting in this strictly dishonourable fashion, doing practically thereby what he had reprimanded Peronella for doing, exactly what he had given his word not to do, and exactly what Peronella had prophesied he would do. Was it that something the girl said had struck him, and he believed in her more than he pretended to do? Was it that he had a spiritual intuition? I fear no. The envelope being open, and he equipped with a slight knowledge of the English tongue, he could not resist the temptation. Was he a fraud? No more than St Peter or King David. He was just that very common phenomenon which novelists refuse to admit—a good man doing a bad action, with no extenuating circumstances.

The letter ran in the original thus (which was not quite as Father Algio closeted in his library with a very old English dictionary rendered it into Alsandrian, but no matter):

MY DEAR SON

"Mr Gaffekin did give me your address which you never thought to send to me or write a line and I think you might have more affection for your old father with one foot in his grave than to leave him and go to foreign parts without a word not to mention robbing me of all my money which I will forgive if you will give back the money at once as I am very poor and the shop going badly, though it was a great sin and shame to rob your father and if you come back I will see you, your loving

"FATHER."

Having made out the rough sense of this the old priest tumbled his head on his beard. A quick psychologist, he knew he had before him a genuine human document, an able logician, he soon deduced the facts of the case from the given data. Then he arose, struck the table violently, swore that divine guidance had prompted him to read the letter (whereby he added the sin of hypocrisy to that of curiosity and misnamed the latter) Not only was the King an impostor, it seemed, but a vulgar thief as well. He sat in his armchair for some time, pondering on what plan he should pursue. At last he left the monastery and, taking the letter and his translation with him, he communicated them in a secret interview to Count Vorza that very night.

And this explains how it was that Count Vorza spent yet a second night pacing up and down his gorgeous courtyard.

CHAPTER XVI

THE COUNTER CONSPIRACY: AN EPISODE IN THE STYLE OF THE WORST WRITERS

Down in a deep dark hole the society plotted a horror.

It was some three weeks after the date of the last chapter that Count Vorza left the palace without giving the customary notification to his august master (who was taking his august siesta), at two o'clock in the afternoon. He passed quickly along, avoiding observation and courting the most devious by-ways, till he came at last to an obscure and squalid doorway at the end of a filthy alley.

"Who is there?" inquired a girl's treble.

"Regnestro."

"Invenu."

He followed into a bare and horrible cellar, damper than a subaqueous vault. This was the Temple of Conspiracy, or shall we say Counter-Conspiracy? correctly chosen, according to all traditions, an utterly unnecessary, even dangerous, choice, for the house of Peronella would have been a far safer resort than this most suspect vault. But no Alsandrian conspirator could have enjoyed himself or felt at ease in less mysterious, less uncomfortable surroundings. Truly the scene was picturesque enough to satisfy the most theatrical appetite: and the motives of the conspirators themselves in plotting against the impostor were various enough to give psychological interest to the melodrama. Dark girder beams projected low, so that the tallest had to stoop: and illumination was produced day and night from a sickly and evil-smelling lamp. Nor were the individuals here assembled less in keeping with the true spirit of second-rate tragedy that pervades the novels of the good old school of Harrison Ainsworth. Here was Cesano, his arms folded, his back to the wall, confident in his power of fascination, aglow with a foretaste of revenge. Peronella had avowed herself sick enough of her English Grocer-King, when Cesano, bursting with Father Algio's tremulous confidences, flung himself at her feet. But there was a fine, large step between hating Norman and loving Cesano: and the girl had by now regained enough spirits to tease quite heartlessly her sombre suitor. She also laughed a little at the conspiracy, but enjoyed being important. She tried at first to give herself the black air of a desolate Ariadne: but soon discarded it in the delights of plotting. She had grown up very swiftly—her beauty was a flourish of trumpets—but how the charm had fled! She was entrusted with the task of admitting the conspirators into the cellar upon the pronouncement of the password. She had taken to practising with a very expensive revolver which she had made Cesano give her, and also to smoking cigarettes, to the distress of Father Algio, who was seated beside her on a packing case. Cesano, whose presence we have remarked, had chosen the darkest corner of the cellar to glower in. Other conspirators prowled round. The lamp was giving out more smoke than ever and the room was stifling. No one could have kept quite sane in such an atmosphere for half-an-hour.

The venerable form of Vorza was greeted with respect and enthusiasm.

"Has anything happened, Duke Vorza?" inquired Peronella, whose modesty was decreasing, before anyone else could get in a word.

"Nothing," said Vorza. "The notice will be round the town in an hour's time: Cuvas has worked well: the whole town will be in the castle square and the usurper will meet his doom."

"What doom?" inquired Peronella, meekly.

"Oh, I doubt if we shall have to take formal proceedings against him. The mob will tear him to pieces, I imagine. Lynch law—those damned republics have taught us something, after all. Ah! is that Cuvas?"

Peronella opened the door and Cuvas, the weary-looking editor of the Alsandrian Gazette, stepped into the room, a stick of a man.

"You have managed splendidly," said Vorza to him.

"I am very tired. You do speak loudly, by the way. I could hear you right outside."

"What, talking about the probable end of our mock King?"

"Yes, and I did not like your talk entirely. Couldn't you ensure his safety? It would be rather a stroke. You see, very luckily the usurper made no attempt against King Andrea but simply put him into an asylum, as we have discovered. Wouldn't it look well in the eyes of Europe if we treated the usurper with the same leniency? Lynching doesn't look well, you know: it doesn't look well."

Cuvas was a man of peace, and not quite such a fool as the others, as will be seen.

"Why, what an absurd idea!" exclaimed the Duke. "You are a queer man, Cuvas, or I would have to call you a coward."

"It would give Alsander such a bad name in the world, brutally to destroy a man who, after all, has done little harm and some good, and we must remember we belong to a civilized State and are now engaged in making history. That is the way things are worked nowadays, you know. Look at Portugal, and Turkey and China. I repeat, the grocer has set a good example."

"You dare praise him for not having killed your lawful King!" cried Father Algio.

"You dare compare the foul deposition of a legitimate monarch to the upsetting of a a low-born, vile, foreign impostor!" cried Vorza.

"Of course not," said Cuvas. "But I deprecate excitement. I deprecate bloodshed. It's the style in which you write your article, not what you say in it, that draws the populace. It's the way you conduct your revolution, not the justice of your cause, that appeals to the diplomats. You must remember that to some people there would be a good deal to be said for the impostor."

"Good things to be said of a grocer!" exclaimed Cesano.

"A Persian cobbler founded Persia's best dynasty," said Cuvas. "And a grocer is not worse than a cobbler. And in England, all things are different: I have heard that in that country grocers may be the friends of Kings and have been ennobled."

"Those English!" groaned Vorza, with contempt. "We are Alsandrians, not Persians, or English, and God be praised! But why to-day of all days do you trouble us with literary dissertations, Cuvas? What has this grocer done that you should defend him before he dies?"

"Well, he has worked already, and worked hard, in the interests of the country. He has begun to dredge the river and pave the streets, and light the town. He is already planning a new railway."

"He?" said Vorza. "Do you think he does anything? He spends half his time shut up with that scoundrelly Jew doctor, whom he would have made Prime Minister if I had let him."

Cuvas thought to himself that Vorza had had many years of power, and yet that more had been done for the country in the last three weeks than during all the years of his regency. However, he had no idea of angering the Count, and held his peace.

"Come, Cuvas," said Father Algio. "Remember what work we have in hand. We have the honour of our country to avenge. We have the Right to fight for. Nothing but death awaits impiety like this. I knew the young man. I could even have loved him once. He may be lowly born, but he looks and acts like a King. I admit it. Truly he has played a fine game with this country with the fiend's aid. But were he my own brother he could not be spared now. He has mocked at religion, fooled the Church, driven out the anointed King, blasphemed the holy oil. His sacrilege is heavy on him, and on this land, and only blood can wipe out our infamy. I am an old man, a feeble man, yet if he were now to come into this room I would tear him with my own hands, and the Queen of the Skies would give me strength to do it. Do not waver, do not flinch, for you are about a high and holy business."

"I wish they would come!" interrupted Peronella, with some impatience, quite irresponsive to this outburst of sacerdotal fervour.

"While we are waiting for the true ruler of this land let us betake ourselves to prayer," continued the priest, not heeding her.

"I hear them!" exclaimed the girl, starting up and leaping to the entrance. There was a sound of a carriage stopping outside and much commotion at the door.

"We have him!" came a reassuring voice, and three guardsmen entered, weary, perspiring, bedraggled and unkempt, bearing with them on a litter none other than the real King Andrea.

"We had to fight our way through the asylum," said the excited guards, in answer to a wind of questions. "There was no other way to get at him. The patients have all escaped and are gibbering in the open fields. Some must have perished: we have had a dreadful time."

They continued vivifying their experiences. Father Algio paid them no attention, but went to the bier and kissed the hand of Andrea, who heard not, felt not, cared not, for he was very sound asleep.

"Where is Makzelo?" asked Cuvas of the guardsmen, cutting short the tale of their heroism.

The guards who had been ordered by Sforelli to catch and imprison Makzelo had never been able to carry out their orders, and that subterranean person had sold Vorza some very decent information at a very decent price.

"Ill, couldn't come," briefly replied the man to whom the question was put: and the others smiled.

"He is not a desperately brave man," said Vorza "But we owe much to his connivance. Ah! his Majesty is opening his eyes!"

And Vorza, who was in general a fairly courageous person, but had not lost that uncanny fear of lunatics to which was due the possibility of the amazing substitution, edged away rapidly.

Royalty opened its eyes, blinked, shut them again, then opened them, stared at Peronella, sat up on his litter, and in a stridently audible voice declared to the assembled company:

"I want her: she must be my Queen!"

His eyes glowed with anticipation. All kept silent, half wondering, half horrified, half amused.

"Come here," continued Andrea, "do come here!"

"The devil take you!" muttered the girl, retreating to the end of the room.

"Do not speak like that to the King," said the priest.

"Come here. I command you. This time I must be obeyed," pursued the old maniac, and a dread sight he was with his stubbly beard and unholy light in his eyes. "They are always taking me away from you! I have waited such a long time—I want to kiss you! Will no one bring her here? This world is all full of traitors and liars."

"Go to him," said Vorza to Peronella. "Cesano, persuade her!"

Peronella's face flushed hot with disgust. The King rose right up and tottered towards her. She instantly put her hand to her girdle and levelled her pistol at him.

"Put him back!" she said, with a quietness almost hysterical.

They had to obey her, well knowing her determined spirit; and fearing the King would become violent the guards strapped him down upon his litter, but fortunately the jolting of the carriage had tired him thoroughly and he slept once more.

"It seems almost a pity," said Cuvas, softly, "to dethrone so active and enterprising an usurper merely to put that driv— that unfortunate King in his place."

He spoke half to himself, but the others heard him. They all began to talk at once with the angry remonstrance of men who feel that they may be in the wrong.

"What is progress?" said Vorza. "We have been happy for a thousand years and will be for another thousand if we are left alone."

"Nothing can come of lies but failure," said Father Algio.

"We are in it to the death now," said Cesano.

"Oh! that is true: so am I. And we have not the slightest prospect of failure. I only said it had a regrettable aspect," said the editor. "And I wondered if any of the people might think so, too, and not be over-anxious to join us when the moment comes!"

"Oh, Cuvas!" said Vorza, in what he took for a light, bantering tone. "You always were a damned old Liberal at heart. But the people of Alsander are staunch and true, and love the old principles, the beauty of their religion, the glories of their city. They do not want their churches desecrated by an unbeliever, their city made boisterous by ugly trains, their pure torrents debased to turn buzzing ma-chines, their river bed all churned up into mud by dredgers, their virgin mountains defiled by smoke and steam."

"But they have shown no discontent," objected the editor, not daring to taunt Vorza for declaring his hatred of the reforms of which he had a few minutes ago delicately suggested himself as the real author.

"You spend all your day on a stool, Cuvas. What do you know about the hearts of our people? You have no time to do anything but transcribe telegrams. The people do not mind, because they are so pleased to have their King returned to sanity. What did I hear an old man say but a few hours ago? He said that no one could become sane straight at once, after all those years; that one might forgive all this reforming nonsense at first, and that he wished anyone might have cured the Sovereign but that hellish Jew of a doctor!"

"Curses on him!" said Father Algio.

"Are you content now, Count Cuvas?" said Vorza.

The title was only in part in jest: ennoblement was the understood reward of complicity.

"You are right: I am well contented," said Cuvas. "I have, of course, some ideas which I do not share with you, but in this business command me. I have joined your conspiracy because I cannot stand immorality and imposture," he added, with dignity. "Still, I can but think it only right to remark once in public—now that it cannot affect our action—what I have so often remarked to you in private—that it would have been no imposture but sound policy to ask old Count Arnolfo whether the rightful heir to the throne, the Princess Ianthe, were not fit to conduct a regency."

Considerable stir was caused by these words of Cuvas, which reflected thoughts which many a conspirator had been waiting for some one else to utter.

"And I have answered you as many times," cried Vorza, turning on him in a veritable fury, "that I have clear evidence that Count Arnolfo's own son was implicated in this dastardly plot. A fine person to ask for information or advice, your Arnolfo! Let us first of all get Andrea safely restored, and then we can talk about a Regency!"

"Well, well," said Cuvas, "you are our leader!" He said it in a tone of resignation which was entirely false, for Cuvas was by no means the simple-souled Conservative-Liberal he seemed. His little speeches, as well as his actions, were a cunning preparation for all eventualities. Two days ago he had sent a trusty messenger to Count Arnolfo to inform him truly not only that the King of Alsander had proved a grocer, but also that the said grocer was in imminent peril of his life and throne.

"Is it nearly time?" called one of the guards. "I hear a noise outside."

Vorza, the only man of the party who possessed a watch (for in Alsander you go by the cathedral bells), looked at it, and cried, "So it is!" The little company hesitated and each of them turned cold for a moment with the terror of excitement. Outside there was a clattering and shouting in the streets, the curious persistent sound of people running all in the same direction.

"Come!" said Vorza. "Where is the wine?"

The wine, or rather spirit, was produced from a bottle in the corner, and poured out into a great bowl, from which each drank in turn, pledging the sleeper in their midst. Then with a shout of "The King! The King!" and with revolvers pointing carelessly aloft and an Alsandrian banner borne by Peronella in the van, the little party streamed out into the alley, and hardly were they in the street when their shout seemed to re-echo all round them and a tremendous cry rose up, thunderous, to heaven, "The King! The King!"

CHAPTER XVII

BATTLE

When you paint a battle-scene let every inch of the foreground be dabbled with blood.
Leonardo da Vinci.

On this very day the King was inspecting the throne-room in the company of Dr Sforelli, who was a person endowed, like most of his race, with a sound artistic instinct. They were gazing on the broken plaster cupids, the faded chinoiseries and singeries, and the immortal lion throne of the Kradenda.

"You must have this renewed," observed Sforelli, stroking his swarthy beard. "It will make a splendid and royal hall."

"Some day," said the King. "Not while there remains a road unpaved or a street lamp unlit in the city of Alsander. Not till my harbour is deep enough for all the navies of the world. And then it shall not be renewed, it shall be cleaned of all the plaster and paint, and left to stand with the ornament of its proportion and no other, save the lion chair of the first Kradenda."

"It rings false, sir. You think you will attain the high ideal of artistic restraint by taking away all the art like your Galsworthy. These little monkeys running up the vine leaves are so well done that I doubt if you would find out of France a painter fit to repair them. Those engaging Chinamen have an idiotic expression which fills the heart with delight. If you do not want them here, where I admit they are out of keeping, you must not destroy them but have them transferred to form a lady's bower, for which some day there will be room in the palace. And when your Majesty has stripped the walls of these pretty things it would be, not merely inaesthetic, but mean-spirited, unroyal, to leave the vast walls white. The great Kradenda would not have left them white, he who himself, the story tells, planned the rose pattern mosaic beneath the cathedral dome. If you say these Chinamen, these monkeys, are vilely out of place, you must find a design that will be in place and keeping."

"Allegorical figures," said the King, sardonically. "Justice with her eyes bandaged, Plenty with a cornucopia, War scowling, Peace smiling, Charity giving away a loaf of bread, Labour with a very red body and big calf muscles smiting at a forge, Commerce watching her ships, Wool Industry watching her sheep, and similar genial devices, such as I believe you see in the offices of banks."

"Do you really think a conventional subject hinders a painter's inspiration?" replied the doctor. "The Italians painted twenty thousand Madonnas and more than half are worth a glance. And if the figure of Peace was tiring in the bank, have you seen the figure of Peace in the Town Hall of Siena? I know of a poor painter starving in Paris who would wreathe your allegory in blazing sunshine by frescoing the walls in little squares; and I know of another, who is starving at Munich, who, by a cunning exaggeration of hollows and curves, would make your figures supernatural and sublime as Michael Angelo's apostles."

"You have made me think, Sforelli," said the King, "that there is just a chance that we may discover a better method even than that. It may be you spoke more truly than you knew when you said that King Kradenda would not have left these walls bare. Who knows if we may not discover under the preserving whitewash of inappreciative fools marvels like those men say await the conquering Crusader who scratches off the Moslem paint from St Sophia? But damn St Sophia! Tell me," continued the King, abruptly changing the subject, "what is the earliest possible date for the projected visit of the Princess Ianthe to my court?"

"As I have informed your Majesty," the doctor courteously replied, "the negotiations are not yet concluded. We hope, however, in about two months' time...."

"It is intolerable!" interrupted the King. "Three weeks have already passed, and now...."

He stopped short on the entry of a lackey who handed him a letter bearing an English postmark.

"That," exclaimed the doctor, "I can recognize from afar as the hand of our friend the old Poet."

Norman tore open the letter, and the lackey having retired, read aloud as follows:—

"DEAR SIR,—

"I hope I am not taking too strange a liberty in writing to you a somewhat personal letter, presuming on a single meeting and a short acquaintance. My only claim upon your attention is that I recommended to you a plan of action which you, subsequently to my advice but of course independently of it, did in the end follow. I would not for a minute presume, sir, to imagine that you were in any way influenced by the random words of one whom you must have taken for a most ridiculous old dotard. It is, indeed, in order to dispel the bad impression I must have made on you by my eccentric dress and appearance that I am writing to you now. May I assure you that these follies were entirely due to some cerebral affection, overpowering indeed, but quite temporary, and probably induced by the extreme heat of the sun? You will remember it was a very hot summer's day when I entered your establishment to purchase some tobacco. May I even go further, and assure you that, apart from these sudden outbreaks and disturbances, I have led a most regular life, was for several years in a city office, and was once mayor of my borough; that I am not addicted to any criminal practices; and that I am, at home, a thoroughly respected and respectful member of civihzed society? But, as I say, I was in a state of mind totally foreign to my saner and better self that afternoon of last summer; and owing, I believe, to the cause above suggested, the unusual, almost volcanic, heat of the day—I had been seeing visions and dreaming dreams after reading Adlington's Apuleius, a book of which I am extremely fond. The sight of an Apuleius between the hands—pardon my bluntness!—of a provision dealer in a small and remote village upset my nerves, and I talked to you, I fear, with an absurd arrogance and an offensive flattery, for which I sincerely apologize.

"I write now, partly, because I am so old that I dare not wait—and, indeed, I think that when you read this letter you may read it as the veritable 'Song of a man that was dead': partly because I feel that a second mental storm is arising within my worn and useless mind, and that I shall not be responsible for what I may shortly do. Finally, permit me to express a hope that you are prospering in the very high social position which you have won—a position in which I am sure your sturdy common sense will stand you in good stead, and that you are keeping in the best possible health.

"With sincere apologies for troubling you,
I remain,
"Your devoted and obedient servant,
"LAURENCE HOPKINSON."

They had no time to comment on this weird letter. As Norman uttered the words "Laurence Hopkinson" it seemed to him that he had started a spell by the very mention of the ungainly name. A hum and murmur came through the open windows: there was a clatter as if the town was waking from its age-long sleep. The inexplicable noise rose louder and louder till it could be distinguished as a roar of men, and the trampling and shouting of a wrathful multitude.

They listened first in wonder, then in alarm, silent. At last Norman cried, "Can you hear what they are shouting?"

"They are crying 'The King! The King!'" observed Sforelli.

"It is not a demonstration in my honour," said Norman, grimly. "Will you come with me and see?"

They crossed the palace courtyard together. Norman remarked with pleasure that the guard were already at the gates.

"There is no danger," said Sforelli, calmly. "All the guards are true as steel. The castle is defended by cannon. The guards know their work well, and we can depend on them to the last breath."

"Viva la rego. Viva nia rego. Viva la rego vera!" thundered the populace. "Viva...." but the iron gates clanged to, and the sound was cut off sharp and the murmur sounded once more dim and far.

A second after, the old Captain of the Palace Guard appeared, a fine white-whiskered old gentleman soldier. He deferentially insisted on leading them into a room above the gateway, whence the crowd could be viewed in all safety. The Captain of the Guard provided them with seats and bowed. "I have to apologize," he said, "for not having come to your side at once, but I thought my first duty was to secure the defences. I can assure your Majesty that there is no danger: and at a word from you we can clear the square."

"Let us give them a chance first," said the King. "I wonder if I could talk to them and find out exactly what they want!"

"They will believe no voice but that of the cannon," said the Captain, gravely, "and the sooner that voice talks the better. There is unfortunately no doubt as to what they want. Look out of this loophole and look at that litter in the centre of the square. They have got Andrea with them, and they mean to reinstate him."

"Well, if we are found out, we are found out," said Norman, with a merry laugh.

"Men that are fools enough to support a cause like theirs," exclaimed Sforelli, "men who prefer to be ruled by a legitimate madman rather than by a true natural King deserve a triple death. Sir, will you not order the Captain to fire?"

"I am in no hurry to shoot down those poor idealists," objected Norman. "For them truth is more important than prosperity: and there is a great deal to be said for their point of view. And you, Captain," he added, turning to the old guardsman at his side, "do you not sympathize in your heart with those tumultuous voices on the square? Are you willing to fire on your fellow-citizens for the sake of a foreign usurper?"

The old Captain drew himself up and saluted. "My King," he said, stiffly. "I hold your life in trust from Princess Ianthe. In fighting for you we fight for her and for her we would blow the whole rabble of Alsander to the moon and ourselves after them. It is she who has commanded us to obey you, and obey you we shall, like the boys obeyed the Old Man of the Mountains, even if you order us to fling ourselves down man by man from the Western Tower. But let me add, Sir, that I and my company do not think that the Princess, whom God preserve, could have chosen a finer ruler for Alsander than the man you have shown yourself to be even in these very few days, my lord the King."

"Captain," replied Norman, "I thank you. I entrust the defence of the Castle entirely to your wisdom. I have only this request to make. I beg of you, let the first shots you fire from our cannon be blank, and the first loaded shells you send pass high above the heads of the crowd; and do not bring out the murderous quickfirers except at the last necessity. Alsandrian blood would weigh heavily upon me, Captain, and not less heavily, I think, on our Royal Mistress."

All the while the King was speaking the savage roar never ceased echoing up through the window—"Fling us down the grocer!—a rope for all traitors!—the river for the foreigner!—the stake for the foreigner!"

The Captain took ceremonious leave in order to attend to his artillery. "I will strictly carry our your Majesty's recommendations," he promised. "We will see if the Castle cannot at least make as much noise as the town."

Left to themselves, Norman and Sforelli observed through an old loophole the turbulent scene on the square below. The hideous mob were swarming before the closed gates and inexpugnable walls: some were trying to collect wood in order to set fire to the Castle, while others were attempting to drag into place some prehistoric guns which the conspirators had unearthed Heaven knows where. Others, again, had diverted their attentions to Sforelli's house, which stood in a corner of the square, and having smashed the windows and burst in the door to a full chorus of Jew-baiting insults, were now proceeding, in order to assuage their disappointment at finding the owner out, to loot each apartment very thoroughly, as could be seen by the phials of acids, books, bottled anatomical specimens and occasional articulated skeletons which came flying out of the upper windows.

"They will be accusing me of ritual murder next!" exclaimed the doctor sorrowfully, as his third and best skeleton came crashing down on the cobbles. "Only I do wish the Captain would hurry up and fire."

At that moment, with tremendous noise and smoke, all the cannons pealed in unison.

"Your blank is being as effective as Napoleon's 'whiff of grape!'" exclaimed Sforelli as soon as the smoke began to roll away. "Look there!"

The crowd were radiating away from the square like a shower of meteors from their centre, seized by a horrible panic. A second harmless broadside of the cannon seemed to have cleared the square completely.

"The square is empty!" cried the King.

"Not quite empty," remarked Sforelli. "What is that over there to the right?"

The King followed the direction of his glance and saw a grisly, battered old sedan chair standing like a dismal island in one corner of the square, beyond the great statue of Kradenda, its tinsel trappings glittering indecently in the sunlight. As he continued to watch it curiously he saw that from the window of this shabby litter a white and twitching face kept bobbing out, a face that wore what could be seen even at that distance to be an irritating expression of mild surprise and general inquiry.

"It is their King," said Sforelli, in deep scorn, looking at the tall and handsome figure beside him, as though he were making a mental comparison.

"This is our time for action," said Norman, glad enough to find a plan for doing something at last. "Our best course will be to go out and bring that poor imbecile into the castle, now that the square is empty, and hold him as a hostage till the leader of this rabble, who I suppose is Vorza, comes in to parley."

And the King, with Sforelli at his heels, rushed down the stairs to the lodge of the gateway where the arms were kept. Having armed himself and his companion with a brace of revolvers, he sent to inform the Captain, and taking with him Sforelli, who refused to leave him, and half-a-dozen men of the Palace Guard, they crossed the square in the direction of the grotesque old sedan chair.

The little company arrived there in a second: not a soul came to oppose them; not a rifle cracked: not a leaf stirred. But when the King was already only a pace or two from the sedan chair, there sprang out suddenly from behind it, like a splendid Amazon, a woman armed. Her hair was loose, her beautiful head poised proudly, her breast half uncovered, her bare right arm swung at her side, and from her right hand gleamed the barrel of a revolver.

Norman sprang back, startled, and hardly recognized the wild apparition.

From within the sedan chair came a dismal moan, "My Queen! my Queen! they have come to take away my Queen!" and the pale head once more came wandering out of the curtains.

"So," said Norman, "that is your new lover, Peronella?"

The girl shivered with disgust at the accusation, but she answered proudly enough: "That is the King of Alsander, you lying English tradesman, and I am here to guard him. You had better have stayed safe in your palace walls. And you had better never have come to Alsander first to betray its women and then to betray its King. And now we shall see who is stronger, you or I!"

"You are growing eloquent, Peronella," said Norman, coolly, "but I have no time to answer your reproaches. I should only like to remark that it is usual to leave a man to guard legitimate monarchs who are in positions of such exceptional difficulty and danger."

"They ran away!" said Peronella, contemptuously.

"Well, we have come to take your charge into the palace. We will not harm him or you. Lift the chair," said the Bang, commanding his guards and turning to the girl he said, "Will you not come, too? You will be safe till this folly is over."

"Thank you for the invitation," retorted the girl. "I am not a Circassian slave!"

And raising her revolver quickly she fired it full in his face. Had not one of the guards, who had been watching her narrowly, knocked up her arm and wrested the weapon from her this story had ended some pages sooner.

"Why did you shoot at him?" said the King, looking again out of his window, dimly comprehending what had happened. "Leave him, my Queen: he is surely my faithful knight who delivered me from the dragon."

But the sound of the shot had its effect. The square was full of eyes and ears. Hundreds saw from their hiding-places how the false King with only four men about him, had come out intending, as they thought, to kill the true King, and they surmised that the great heroine, the divine Peronella, for whom they were ready to die a thousand deaths, was in danger. And they also observed, in quick whispers, one to another, that if the Englishman were in the square the cannon could not be fired at them for fear of killing him too. Also they were beginning to realize that no one had been hurt by the last firing of the said cannon, and one voluble fellow swore that to his personal knowledge the cannons were only what he called salute cannons, and there was no ammunition in the Castle. These several considerations ran in whispers from mouth to mouth and fanned the flickering courage of the Legitimists, and, a thousand to eight, they rushed back into the square they had so speedily deserted ten minutes ago with a shout of triumph. Seeing the deadly peril of their master and the impossibility of using their cannon effectively, the Palace Guards instantly made a sortie under the command of the old Captain, and in a few seconds a savage fight was raging all round the statue of Kradenda.

Peronella, snatched away from the guardsman who had disarmed her by the rude hands of passionate rescuers, was born aloft, waving in her hand, in place of the ravished revolver, a frantic, bloody sword wherewith the gallant Cesano, with a mighty sweep, had just slashed off the arm of one of the guards. The odds for the moment were tremendous against the Palace. There were only ten men left to guard the door, which could not be shut for fear of barring the escape of the others; and fifty other guards were pushing their way towards Norman and his supporters—an all but hopeless task—for even their discipline and superior weapons were useless against a mad mob of a thousand men.

But a diversion came from an unexpected quarter. The tumult had strangely affected Andrea and strange phantoms were dancing down the crooked corridors of his mind. For him the noise of the sorry tumult became the noise of his battle, and the pushing, shuffling throng behind him were his trampling warriors serried in their thousands. He remembered his ancestry and heard the voice of him who was called Iron. Brave words from old and musty books fanned the sleeping fires of his manhood; lovely forms of long dead women, memories of tattered tapestries and dim old paintings sailed before his dazzled, visionary eyes. But clearest and fairest he saw, as it were, amongst all those phantoms one figure—passionately real—the figure of Peronella waving her bloodstained sword. Why had they taken her away? The enemy had taken her, and she was calling to him for aid. He could not but obey the summons of her distressed beauty, perfect knight of chivalry that he was.

"At them, my men!" he cried. "Save the Queen! Follow me!"

And he leapt out of his couch, tugging at the sword wherewith the conspirators had adorned him, lest he should be too pitiable a sight, even for loyalists. It had been fastened into its scabbard for security, but wrenching scabbard and all from his belt he dealt such a shattering blow on the head of the nearest bystander that the scabbard flew off along a jet of blood, and in an instant the King was dealing round him madly with his naked sword. Three of his loyal subjects became martyrs to their cause by mistake before anyone could realize danger: others fled before him; In another second he would have clasped Peronella in his arms, but her attendant swains bore her to safety behind the great statue of Kradenda, which stood proudly in the centre of the square, above all the turmoil.

The King saw an old helmeted warrior thrice the size of life, standing between him and his beloved. He knew not it was his ancestor, suspected not that it was stone. He dealt the statue a furious blow with his sword, and his sword fell shattered at his feet. He leapt on to the statue and clutched it round the neck. It fell over him. In one mass on the ground, all crushed and broken, lay together the statue of Kradenda and the body of Andrea.

Thus, in the temporary realization of the chivalrous ideal, his shattered sword stained with foolish blood, was Andrea the Mad, for nine years King of Alsander, killed by the statue of his celebrated ancestor. And as to what madness is, and whether we are mad and they are sane, that is a long discussion, but it is certain that it is an ill thing for the sane to rule the mad, or the mad the sane. And it is known that there was a light of glory and happiness shining in Andrea's eyes at the moment of his death such as none of us will ever show when we look into the mouth of the pit: and it may be his life was well worth while, to attain that moment.

However, this strange incident and the very detonation of the statue's fall, seemed only to incite the fury of the mob. With a blind rush they surrounded Norman's little company, thereby cutting them off hopelessly from the thirty or forty Palace Guards who were passionately struggling to the rescue. Had the crowd been properly armed, Norman and his friends would have been annihilated at once: but fortunately only a few of the populace had revolvers and the rest, equipped only with mattocks and stones, took good care to keep out of range of the swords of the guardsmen, and dreaded still more than those circling swords the unpleasantly quick and accurate automatic pistols with which the Palace fought. Moreover, Norman's band had gained great heart from the gallant behaviour of the little wizened Cassolis and four other members of the Advancement Association who, not being known participants of the conspiracy, pushed their way through the seething masses to the King's side, and on their arrival suddenly whipped out their revolvers and fired point plank at the assailants.[1]

But the respite was a short one; the multitude seemed to swell above them like a monstrous wave. Stones wrenched from the cobbled ground hailed round the devoted band, stray bullets pinged and splashed on the pedestal of the fallen statue against which, above the very body of Andrea, they had set their backs for a last stand. At all events they were, in the old phrase, selling their lives dearly. Of the bodies that lay around them they constructed a bleeding and quivering rampart, on the summit of which one of the guards, wounded to death, heroically laid himself to die.

It was now that Vorza, with that popular heroine Peronella at his side, rallied his forces for a vigorous onset, and the reactionary statesman, espying the swarthy head of Sforelli towering over the fight, screamed out in a passion, "Cut down that cowardly Jew!"

"I'll give you cowardly Jew!" roared Sforelli in answer, and rushing out from behind that crimson fleshy fortification of theirs he flung through the crowd straight at their startled leader. All fell back in terror from his mad attack. Sforelli reached his goal in a flash and seized Vorza lightly as it seemed by the shoulders. The next instant all that statesmanship went hurtling over the heads of the crowd; and the next, that brain, which had furnished so much valuable counsel to the citizens of Alsander, was spilt over the stony floor. Norman, for all his astonishment, realized in a flash at the same moment what master of the art had taught the frail Princess the trick that had once laid him low on the floor of the curiosity shop, a woman's victim.

But the wrestler's skill could no further avail Sforelli; he paid for his vengeance with his life. He fell, literally bashed to death, and his excellent soul, released from the unprepossessing body, descended to whatever dark abode is destined for the disciples of Voltaire, at the very moment that Vorza's (for Vorza never stirred again) was carried off by angels.

Death, shame to tell, did not rescue the doctor's battered body from the insults of the populace, and among that evil populace conspicuous was Peronella, delirious at the sight of pain and blood, like other fighting women of history of whom record tells. Cesano saw with horror her dripping arms and the vile glitter in her eyes. Good honest fellow that he was, beneath all his extravagances, he feared for her reason and was ashamed for her womanhood. Little did that lover care at that moment for foolish Conspiracy, or the leaderless crowd that gaped around him: he seized Peronella, swung her roughly from the ground and bore her out of the fray.

Short enough was the relief which the spectacular death of the opposing leader afforded to the Palace, but a relief it was. For a full minute's space the shepherdless rabble recoiled, and the now decimated party of the Palace Guards, fighting their way towards the centre of the square, took heart of grace. Heavily they laid on around them, with much hacking and hewing at hands and heads and frequent hamstringing of their terrified adversaries. Blood rained down from their swords like heavy snow melting from the trees in early spring. But before they had made twenty yards of headway the courage and fanatic zeal of Father Algio had rendered even this great effort vain. Raising a silver cross on high he called "Vengeance for the King" with such fury that the whole crowd took up the shout and a deafening "Vengeance" boomed over the square like a blast of the North wind. Those who surrounded the fiery-eyed old priest made a dash at the ghastly barricade and began tearing it down. Then indeed Norman, thrice wounded, gasping, slipping on blood and tattered flesh, expected the sudden darkness; and in his extremity, as though to reply to, the crowd's yell for vengeance, he could not but cry aloud the name that for him evoked all the joy of living. Fiercely enough his followers took up the cry, shouting, with uplifted swords, "Ianthe and for Ianthe!" making the name of their Lady ring and ring out again with all the passion of men about to die.

Suddenly, at that very minute, with such weird effect that some of the little band dreamt they had died already, there pealed through the Castle square what seemed the enchanted answer of their shouting, not that savage cry of vengeance, but a yet stranger, a yet wilder tumult,—the blowing of a hundred horns with rattling hoof-beats to mark the measure. And forthwith from the great North Road poured into the square at full gallop, their horses foaming and steaming, a troop of cavalry in the radiant panoply of the Royal Alsandrian Frontier Guard. In the hush caused by their astounding entry their burly colonel put up a megaphone and bawled, "Cease fire in the name of the Princess! All fighting to cease!" However, without waiting for this command to take effect the troopers laid on with their long whips and drove back the rabble to one corner of the square, at the same time forming guard round Norman and their fellow soldiers of the Palace.

The Englishman and his followers leant back half dead against the blood-stained marble, stunned by this deliverance, too weak to ask one question of their rescuers. And then down into the midst of the square towards them, escorted by one whom many knew to be the old Count Arnolfo, on a great glistening black horse, rode the Princess Ianthe.

"And where," she cried, "is the King of Alsander?" and at the very moment of her asking her eyes lighted full on Norman.

She was bronze helmeted, a very Athena, and dressed in the gold and green uniform of the Alsandrian Riders, but it was Ianthe the woman who commanded the square, calling for her King. Her face indeed still looked boyish enough, with her hair half hidden by the flashing helmet; and her young body looked so slim in the handsome uniform that it might well have been a lad's. The large dark eyes, aglow with intelligence, had dominated the face of the boy; but as she caught sight of Norman she smiled gently: and it was the strange smiling of her perfect mouth that revealed Ianthe an enchantress among women. That smile, which da Vinci caught years ago and fixed in a picture whose destiny has proved as restless as its charm—the smile of the boy-like Renaissance women—of the women who knew art and history and secrets beautiful and tragic which have perished with their smiles—such a smile played over the face of Ianthe as she bent her eyes down to her wounded lover, leaning wearily on his dripping sword. And he, looking up, saw in amaze the new apparition of her splendour—that special and rare beauty of a woman whose life is ruled by passionate intelligence: and he cried out, "O Queen of Alsander!" and as she dismounted flung his sword on the ground before her.

Seeing this parley of the Princess and the Impostor some of the bewildered crowd murmured, and one man shouted, "The King of Alsander is lying dead at your feet!"

"Ah!" muttered Ianthe, shuddering as she looked at the staring head beneath her, "is that Andrea? That my kinsman?"

"He fought with the statue till it fell on him and slew him," explained Cassolis briefly. "Sforelli killed Vorza and himself perished, and your Majesty is now by undisputed title Queen of Alsander."

"If Vorza is dead who leads this mob?" inquired the grey old Count Arnolfo.

"A fanatic priest," some one replied.

"Bring him before us," the Count commanded.

He came before them, cross in hand, a black cowled, black frocked, frost bearded old monk with mad blue eyes, and before anyone had spoken, he flung himself on his knees before Ianthe.

"Queen of Alsander," he cried, pointing to Norman, "if this man was known to you, was crowned with your connivance, has been fighting in your name, why did you not tell your faithful people of Alsander?"

"And why," rejoined the Princess in clear tones that could be heard all over the square, "when you and your friends discovered that the King was not Andrea, did you send no word to me, but, without the authority of the Royal Family of Alsander, plotted by yourselves like anarchists?"

"And why," said Norman, "did you, again like anarchists, send no summons to the Palace, but, without formally demanding my abdication, set your rabble on me and my followers like a pack of starving curs? It had been arranged that on an emergency you should have been told the truth. But you gave us no chance, and the blood of my brave men and of those poor fools and of your King himself is on the heads of your conspirators."

"There is but one answer to your question and you know it," said old Count Arnolfo, "and that is that Vorza your dead leader was a traitor, an ambitious traitor, and a vile traitor!"

But the Princess cut them short. "Set me on the pedestal where stood the statue of my ancestor," she cried, "and the King beside me. Thence I will address Alsander!" And on to the pedestal she sprang with easy grace, but the King, for all that an old soldier had roughly staunched his wounds, had to be lifted, weak and fainting, to her side. "Courage, my lover," she whispered, as she bent to raise him. "Do I forget that you are wounded, that you are weary? But stand up now for the sake of Alsander, and for a moment face these simple folk with me."

Straight and stiff he stood and deadly pale, leaning on her arm while she in ringing tones spake to her people.

"I," she said, "since the King Andrea is dead, am by divine right and undisputed title Queen of Alsander. From you who, without deigning to consult me, have fought for the divine right of my house, utter obedience and submission I expect. I do as I choose, I say as I choose, I dispose of Alsander as I choose, and I make King thereof the man I choose, and that King is at my side. If he is a foreigner so was the great Kradenda: if he is of lowly birth, so, too, was that founder of all Alsander's fortune, in the place of whose monument, destroyed by and destroyer of my unhappy kinsmen, we now stand together. May the omen which was disastrous for him be propitious for us! Now you may know that this very night will be celebrated in the Castle privately, out of respect for my dead kinsman, my union with the already consecrated King whom you have tried so savagely to kill. And expect no further excuse or explanation from me; for you have behaved like fools, O people of Alsander, and had I not been warned just in time of what was brewing by the only loyal man in your conspiracy, irreparable disaster would have befallen the State. And now my soldiers will guard and prepare for interment with all honour the remains of King Andrea, of that good patriot Sforelli, and of those brave soldiers who have perished in this miserable tumult. Those of you who have your own dead on this square may remain to attend them unmolested; but the rest of you must disperse at once and quietly to your several homes."

The half understanding populace listened in sullen silence to these bitter and uncompromising words. But an old shoemaker who stood in the front rank of the crowd, his dim eyes enchanted and his aged heart fired by the beauty and fearlessness of the young Queen, cried out: "Treat us as you will, Queen Ianthe of Alsander, but do not be angry with your people: for we have been mightily deceived."

The Princess was moved. "You were led by an evil shepherd," she replied, "who forced me to deceive you. But love for the people of Alsander is branded on my heart—and on the King's."

"Then let us cheer," shouted the old shoemaker, shaking his grizzled locks toward the crowd, "for the Queen—and for the King of Alsander!"

We leave them there, the Mistress and the Captain of a little ship of State, and only ask, before we turn to the Epilogue in Blaindon—But what of Peronella? Did Cesano thrash the nonsense out of her in good Alsandrian fashion, wed her, and live happily ever after, peopling with troops of swarthy children some mountain cottage in a foreign land? Or did he quail before her flashing eyes, dismissed for ever, and is that darker fancy true that it is she whom men call the Blood-red Rose from the cabins of Moscow to the cabarets of Montmartre, she for whom many have died, she who they say has ordered the death of legions in her fierce hatred of Kings and the minions of Kings? Only this is certain, that neither she nor her lover were ever seen again in that fantastic town, Alsander.

[1] I much regret my inability to bring in at this juncture our old friend the British Consul at Alsander. Unfortunately he was not in town, but had taken advantage of a well-earned holiday to go shooting in the mountains. Had he been in Alsander there is little doubt but that he would have pushed through the crowd in his uniform to claim and protect Norman as a British subject.

CHAPTER XVIII

THE POET VISITS BLAINDON ONCE MORE, AND TAKES JOHN GAFFEKIN TO THE SEASHORE WHERE A MIRACLE OCCURS

... les hommes aux yeux verts ... ceux-là qui aiment la mer, la mer immense, tumultueuse et verte, l'eau informe et multiforme.
Baudelaire.

Vives autem beautus, vives in mea tutela gloriosus, et cum spatium saeculi tui permensus ad inferos demearis ibi quoque in ipso subterraneo semirutundo me ... videbis Acherontis tenebris interlucentum, Stygiisque penetralibus regnantem.
Isis to Lucius in the "Golden Ass."

John Gaffekin, weary of this world, left his invalid mother asleep, in charge of the nurse, and walked down into Blaindon after a miserable meal. His mother's health was worse, his prospects gloomy; his life had become very friendless since Norman went abroad. From the latter, moreover, he had had no news for months.

The night was clear and pleasant, but to a lonely man the far-shining brilliance of the Blaindon Arms appeared more pleasant still: and so he turned on his heel and swung in through the unaccustomed door.

"Why, bless me, Mr Gaffekin," said Nancy, "it's a long time since you've been in."

"It is, indeed, Nancy. How's life?"

"Oh, just as usual, Mr Gaffekin, thank you. Have you heard from Mr Price again?"

"Not a word," said John. "Not a single word since last summer."

"Now, that's odd, sir," said Peter Smith, "very odd."

"I tell you what," said Thomas Bodkin, the sexton, with prodigious wisdom, "he's fallen in love."

"He wasn't much that sort, Mr Bodkin," said Nancy, with a little sigh. It pleased her to imagine that her heart was broken.

"Damned silly," said old Canthrop. "Damned silly. Never tould his feyther."

"And the old man so cut up about it," said Peter Smith.

"Yes," said John. "Didn't get back to business for nearly a week."

"Ah, it's curious to think of him so far away," said Nancy. "Out there in Aljanda. That is, if he wasn't killed in the row."

"Ah, if...." said the sexton ominously.

The Daily Mail had contained one day a few months ago a small paragraph which had caused quite an excitement in the village of Blaindon, reporting "considerable fermentation in the little State of Alsander." But the succeeding numbers had no further information on the subject, being well stocked with letters answering the grave question "Is the stage immoral?" which the great paper had proposed to itself with typical earnestness and audacity. The inhabitants of Blaindon, however, were not deterred by the meagreness of the data from an almost daily discussion as to whether their fellow townsman had perished.

"You cheer up, Nancy," said John Oggs, who was the sexton's opponent in the controversy. "Price is all right, and he'll turn up again one of these days, all boiled yellow by the sun."

"What a strange thing Life is," said Nancy.

"A strange thing indeed," said old Canthrop. "A strange thing."

"The sun makes one red, not yellow," said the sexton. "But it's small colour he's showing now, poor boy, I can tell you. In them furrin parts knives aint reserved for cheese. And he'd have written for sure."

"Ah, sexton," said John to escape the perpetual topic, "I can see you're a man of ideas."

"Well, Mr Gaffekin, I may not have been to Oxford, as I say, but I does think. As I said to Parson once before a burial. 'You and I, sir,' I said, 'are thinking men.' It goes with the business."

"It must be dreadful work," said John Oggs. "Digging holes for dead men. Well, we must all go under."

"Ay, indeed," said old Canthrop.

"Don't speak from the bottom of your throat like that," said Peter Smith. "It gives me the horrors, with all this talk about death and all."

"Death should not give anyone the horrors," said the sexton, who attended church regularly. "It is but the Portal, Of a better life beyond."

"But it's rather nice to have the horrors sometimes," came Nancy's voice from behind the bar. "I wonder why!"

"Not but what," continued the sexton, "it is not excusable now for me. For my work is very sad and awesome indeed."

The sexton had never before been so impressed with the conversational advantage of his lugubrious occupation, and he determined to make up for lost opportunities.

"I believe you, sexton," said Peter Smith,

"Some of them as I've buried was all young and blooming, and others were ever so old, nearly as old as Canthrop yonder."

"Don't talk like that," said the patriarch, hoarsely. "Ye make me afeard."

"I wonder what it is to-night," said a labourer in the corner who had hitherto drunk in silence, "that makes you all talk as if you couldn't say what you meant."

"Perhaps a man is being hanged," said the sexton.

"Poor fellow!" said Nancy.

"I feel queer to-night," drawled old Canthrop. "But I don't know why that is. What is it makes it so?"

"The moon, old man, the moon."

The company started with fear at the sound of this strange voice, turned round, and with blanched faces beheld the figure of an old man framed in the doorway, with the silver light creeping along his hoary beard, and over his unprecedented clothes. For the stranger was clothed in what appeared to be a white woollen dressing-gown, with a purple border, and he had sandals on his feet. He wore no hat, and his snowy hair waved gently in the radiance of the gaslight. He walked forward amid a dead silence, and laid his hand on old Canthrop's shoulder.

"Yes, old comrade in a life of folly," he cried. "The moon is full to-night, and you know it is her fault. Hers are the fiery drops that make your eyes water and my eyes shine. I, to whom she has revealed her secret springs of knowledge and beauty, you, who have not fifty words to your tongue—I, who feel her gentle influence pervading forest and meadow, tower and town, you, who feel only the terror of her nocturnal power that brings you to your fellows, you, the village dotard, I, the king of the world; we have one mother, old man, and that's the Moon! You see and fear the great white spaces that flit before your eyes; I know and love her cloudy caverns of mystery and wonder."

"Who are you?" whispered old Canthrop. "Go away!"

"A minute, a minute. I am what you will, Death, Destiny, a Poet. Is John Gaffekin here?"

"Are you...." began John.

"I am the same. Ask nothing more. My dear—a drink round to all, for our farewell."

The Poet looked round, smiling at the solemn and pale faces, at the trembling hands of those that proposed his health. Then, linking his arm through John's, he took him out into the street.

"Come with me," said the Poet, "we will go to old William Price's shop."

After five minutes' walk in a silence which John Gaffekin somehow did not wish to break they arrived outside the little square brick house which was dark, silent and shuttered fast. In front of it the last gas-lamp in Blaindon glimmered in the wind-driven moon-rays.

"Call the old man," ordered the Poet.

John Gaffekin banged violently at the door and shouted: "Mr Price! Mr Price!"

"Eh, what's up the deuce and all?" came a loud but sleepy voice from the first floor. A match was struck, a light glimmered through the bars, the shutters creaked open and old Mr Price popped his nightcap out of the window.

"News from your son," cried the Poet cheerfully.

"Eh, is that anything to jump a man up for in the dead o' night?" retorted the old man, cursing under his breath. "I was feared of a smoky black beggaring fire at the least, I was. What the devil do I care about the young rip? He owes me a hundred pound, he do, and I wrote him, but he never sent back a penny nor a post-card."

"You're a nice, pretty father," exclaimed the Poet. "I've got your hundred in my pocket."

"I'll come down to you and Mr Gaffekin," said William Price very civilly.

"No you won't," retorted the Poet, "you should have come down before. You'll stay right where you are and answer me some questions I have in my head to ask you. And if you budge from that window you sha'n't have a groat nor a tizzy of all your hundred pounds."

"It's cold-here," grumbled Mr Price, churlishly, flapping his arms across his chest. "What d'yer want to know?"

"Why, first of all, tell me why you never go out of nights?" cried the Poet.

"What's that to you?" bawled back the old man.

"And tell me, tell me, William Price, who was the mother of your son?" the Poet shouted.

"What in Hell or under it is that to you?" came in very full-throated accents from the open window.

"Why is your bedstead all made of wood?" thundered the relentless Poet in stentorian tones.

"Hey, stop that!" cried the voice from the window.

But the Poet continued his questions unperturbed.

"Why have you half forgotten your own son, William Price? Why do you sleep all day, Father William, and pretend to be more stupid than the grave? Do you think a Poet cannot see through the film you cast over your happy eyes?"

"Eh, what are you driving at?" exclaimed Sir Price in a voice no longer angry but rather tremulous.

"Who are your guests to-night, old man, who are your guests to-night?" yelled the Poet, positively dancing with malicious satisfaction.

"Why, be you one of them that know?" cried the old man in a new tone of something like awe and something like fellowship.

"I am one of the chief of those that know," replied the Poet; "for me shutters unbar, for me the music pipes, and even my companion for all he can wrap his soul up in the wisdom of Oxford town shall see the fairies haunting."

"What!" said John.

But the Poet urbanely continued: "I'm forgetting those hundred pounds," and taking out a sheaf of banknotes from a vast white pocket like a snow-cavern he crumpled them into a ball and hurled them at one of the barred shutters.

The shutter opened to let the packet pass.

"Money, my friend," observed the Poet tranquilly, "opens all doors."

A soft peal of very quiet laughter filled the little house and all the other shutters opened to a thin music: room after room flashed into light as though so many plays were starting on so many miniature stages with all the shadows flying to the roof: and one by one the half naked little women of the wild crept out of hiding and began their dance. And through it all as though it meant nothing for him, though his room was flashing from hue to hue like a transformation scene and an enchanting person had her arms around his neck, old Price bawled down: "Well, what of Norman?"

"He has become King of that country and wedded to its Queen," roared the Poet.

"I always said he was a sound practical fellow without an idea in his head," remarked William Price with serene philosophy.

"Like most of the Half-Race," assented the Poet.

"But we filled his bottle with luck," trilled the silvery lady upstairs.

"And his countenance with beauty," replied the Poet. "Well, we really must be off now. Good-bye to you all, and a pleasant evening!"

Laughing good-byes rippled back at him from all over the house like the jingling of toy harness bells.

"Let us walk down to the sea," said the Poet, turning to go. "How far is it to the sea, John?"

"Ten miles."

"And by which road?"

"Straight on."

"Ah, yes," said the Poet, setting off at a swinging pace, "it is the road by which first I came to Blaindon."

But before they had gone many yards John heard his name called and stood still. Down through the moonlight glided as it might be a wingless angel and by his side there stood the fairy of the upper window.

"John," she said, "when you see my son again give him this kiss."

And kissing him she floated away.

The Poet who had gone ahead, waited for John to come up.

"But I must go back to my mother," the young man protested, as though a glimpse of the unmagical past had driven a sword through his mind. "She is very ill."

"I fear she will die within the week," replied the Poet, "but I inquired at your house on the way to the Blaindon Arms and learnt that to-night she is happily asleep and will not need you. When you are alone in the world, John, you must go to Norman to give him his mother's kiss and help him through days of trouble. It's no easy game even in a little country, even with a born Queen, even with the Immortals helping—the game of King."

He said no more. The two went on together on the road leading to the sea, without another word, for miles. John dared not speak; he was half delirious with the silence; the dread prediction of his mother's death, the wild story about his friend, rang in his ears; the house of the Fairies danced before his eyes; and he feared his fateful companion. The wizard forms of the hedges threatened John Gaffekin, the harvest moon, golden and vast, seemed to shine hot upon his hatless brow. He kept comparing the trickling of the roadside brook to the trickling of the little thoughts in his head; he could not get rid of this grotesque comparison, and grew more afraid. At last the poet broke the silence.

"Are you lonely, John?" he said. "Or have you found women after your desire?"

"Women?" said John. "I never cared for any woman but for my mother. I have one friend far away of whom you tell me news I cannot understand. I have known many men at Oxford—good athletes or great wits. But I shall never make another friend like him. I shall certainly seek him out if what you predict falls true. I am indeed lonely."

They were silent again. They had now come to brackish marshes, and to a land of dizzy vapours. The wind blew harder from the sea, singing like a hero, bringing with it a salt and pungent odour. The poet linked his arm with the young man's as though to protect him from the evil spells of night.

"Take heart, my friend," said he. "You have years of glorious life before you, and it is a splendid night for visions."

John suddenly stopped, swung round to face the old man, and began speaking hurriedly, gasping for breath before each phrase.

"What has happened?" he cried. "Why am I here? Who are you? An hour or two ago I was just an unhappy man, rather lonely, with a mother lying ill. Now, you tell me my mother will die, and you tell me news about my friend too wild for a sober man to repeat; you have already shown me that which I feared to see, and now, as though it were not sufficient, you say the night is propitious for visions. I am so distressed in mind that I cannot talk properly; the words get inverted, the world reels like a decadent's dream, my head is turning with it, and I keep on feeling a sort of brook trickling. What are you doing in that white coat? Who are you? Tell me who you are."

John raised his voice to the pitch of anger at the end, wroth that this mysterious being should cross his path "fantasia, non homo."

"Be calm, my friend: all is well; you are not used to the extensions of Reality, that is all. I do not want to take advantage of the night. Behold we have arrived at the seashore. Leave me now, friend of Norman! Go on to that distant rock, and watch. You may see what is to be seen. But do not profane the silence of the moonlight."

And he waved his hands in front of John's bewildered eyes as he chanted low the injunction.

John obeyed him as by constraint, and watched from a rock some hundred yards away.

The old man made ablutions in the sea and began to intone his prayer.

"Thou who appearest in the waves of water, of wind and of fire, Queen who with special majesty dost sway the minds of men, the beasts and cattle and all the moving substance of the thundering world, appear to me, be mine, be myself: show the lucid sign upon thy brows: grant me the reward for faithful service: let me hear once again from those immortal lips thy ancient promise, that in the pit of Acheron, yea, even there, thou wilt be shining among the thoughtless dead. Thou art and art not the great Cytherean, mother of the world, thou art and art not Artemis, the virgin of the forests, the huntress, thou art and art not Pallas, to whom the snake has told his story, thou art and art not her to whom sailors pray in the still waters of the middle sea: it may be the Egyptians knew thee by thy name: it may be thou art the mother of Christians in the South. Thou art in me but thou art not what I am! I salute thee!"

John saw the old man fling off his white mantle: an instant after it was in flames: Then he thought he saw him rise naked among the flames and run toward the sea with a silver disc shining on his breast: and he began to swim out along the track of the moon. Then he saw the great full moon burst into a shower of stars and fall into the sea, and a white woman rose, huge and glorious, from the waves, with a horned helmet on her brow and spread over the sky like light till she filled the world. Then the treble octave was sounded all through the universe, and he fell senseless.

He awoke hours later, but saw nothing save a wet sea rolling in the dawn.

AN ESSAY ON JAMES LEROY FLECKER by JC SQUIRE

In person Flecker was tall, with blue eyes, black, straight hair, and dark complexion. There was a tinge of the East in his appearance, and his habitual expression was a curious blend of the sardonic and the gentle. Until illness incapacitated him he was physically quite active, but his principal amusement was conversation, of which he never tired. He felt acutely the loss of good talk during his years abroad, in Syria especially. He was sociable, and enjoyed meeting and talking with crowds of people; but he had few intimate friends at Oxford, and, after he left England, little opportunity of making any. One of the few, Mr. Frank Savery, now of the British Legation, Berne, sends the following notes:

"My acquaintance with him began in January 1901, when he was a lanky, precocious boy of sixteen, and lasted, with long interruptions, until his death. His fate took him to the Near East, mine took me to Germany: for this reason we never met from 1908 to 1914, though we never ceased to correspond. Largely because our intercourse was thus broken, I believe that I am better able to appreciate the changes which his character underwent in the latter years of his life than those who never lost sight of him for more than a few months at a time.

"It was at Oxford that I first came to know him intimately. He was extraordinarily undeveloped, even for an English Public School boy, when he first went up in 1902. He already wrote verses—with an appalling facility that for several years made me doubt his talent. He imitated with enthusiasm and without discrimination, and, the taste in those long-gone days being for Oscar Wilde's early verse and Swinburne's complacent swing, he turned out a good deal of decadent stuff, that was, I am convinced, not much better than the rubbish written by the rest of his generation at Oxford. What interested me in Flecker in those days was the strange contrast between the man—or rather the boy—and his work. Cultured Oxford in general, I should add, was not very productive at that time: a sonnet a month was about the maximum output of the lights of Balliol. The general style of literature in favour at the time did not lend itself to a generous outpouring. Hence there was a certain piquancy in the exuberant flow of passionate verse which issued from Flecker's ever-ready pen in spite of his entire innocence of any experience whatever.

"Furthermore, he was a wit—a great wit, I used to think, but no humorist—and, like most wits, he was combative.

He talked best when some one baited him. At last it got to be quite the fashion in Oxford to ask Flecker to luncheon and dinner-parties—simply in order to talk. The sport he afforded was usually excellent…. Looking back on it now, I believe I was right in thinking that in those days he had no humour (there is very little humour in Oxford); nor am I so entirely sure that his wit was bad. I had, at any rate, a growing feeling that, in spite of his immaturity and occasional bad taste, he was the most important of any of us: his immense productiveness was, I vaguely but rightly felt, better and more valuable than our finicky and sterile good taste.

"By 1906 he had developed greatly—largely thanks to the companionship of an Oxford friend whom, in spite of long absence and occasional estrangements, he loved deeply till the end of his life. Even his decadent poems had improved: poor as are most of the poems in 'The Bridge of Fire,' they are almost all above the level of Oxford poetry, and there are occasional verses which forecast some of his mature work. Thus I still think that the title-poem itself is a rather remarkable achievement for a young man and not without a certain largeness of vision. The mention of this poem reminds me of an episode which well illustrates the light-heartedness which at that time distinguished the self-styled 'lean and swarthy poet of despair.' I was sitting with him and another friend in his rooms one day—early in 1906, I think—when he announced that he was going to publish a volume of poems. 'What shall I call it?' he asked. We had made many suggestions, mostly pointless, and almost all, I have no doubt, indecent, when Flecker suddenly exclaimed: 'I'll call it "The Bridge of Fire," and I'll write a poem with that name and put it in the middle of the book instead of the beginning. That'll be original and symbolic too.' We then debated the not unimportant question of what 'The Bridge of Fire' would be about. At midnight we parted, the question still unsettled. Flecker, however, remarked cheerfully that it did not much matter—it was a jolly good title and he'd easily be able to think of a poem to suit it.

"Flecker always cherished a great love for Oxford: he had loved it as an undergraduate, and afterwards not even the magic of the Greek seas, deeply as he felt it, ever made him forget his first university town. But on the whole I think that Cambridge, where he went to study Oriental languages in preparation for his consular career, did more for him. I only visited him once there—in November 1908, I think—but I had the distinct impression that he was more independent than he had been at Oxford. He was writing the first long version—that is to say, the third actual draft—of the 'King of Alsander.' Incidentally he had spoilt the tale, for the time being, by introducing a preposterous sentimental conclusion, a departure to unknown lands, if I remember rightly, with the peasant-maid, who had not yet been deposed, as she was later on, from her original position of heroine.

"And now follow the years in which my knowledge of Flecker is drawn only from a desultory correspondence. I should like to quote from some of the letters he wrote me, but, alas, they are in Munich with all my books and papers. He wrote to me at length whenever he had a big literary work on hand; otherwise an occasional post card sufficed, for he was a man who never put either news or gossip into his letters. I knew of his marriage; I knew that his literary judgment, as expressed in his letters and exemplified in his writings, had improved suddenly and phenomenally. That was all.

"At last his health finally collapsed and he came to Switzerland. It was at Locarno, in May 1914, that I saw him again. He was very ill, coughed continually, and did not, I think, ever go out during the whole fortnight I spent with him. He had matured even more than I had expected....

"He was very cheerful that spring at Locarno—cheerful, not extravagantly optimistic, as is the way of consumptives. I think he hardly ever mentioned his illness to me, and there was certainly at that time nothing querulous about him. His judgment was very sound, not only on books but also on men. He confessed that he had not greatly liked the East—always excepting, of course, Greece—and that his intercourse with Mohammedans had led him to find more good in Christianity than he had previously suspected. I gathered that he had liked his work as Consul, and he once said to me that he was very proud of having been a good businesslike official, thereby disposing, in his case at any rate, the time-honoured conception of the poet as an unpractical dreamer. He was certainly no mere dreamer at any period of his life; he appreciated beauty with extraordinary keenness, but, like a true poet, he was never contented with mere appreciation. He was determined to make his vision as clear to others as it was to himself.

"I saw Flecker once more, in December 1914. He was already visibly dying, and at times growing weakness numbed his faculties. But he was determined to do two things—to complete his poem, 'The Burial in England,' and to put his business affairs into the hands of a competent literary agent. The letters and memoranda on the latter subject which he dictated to me were admirably lucid, and I remember that, when I came to read them through afterwards, I found there was hardly a word which needed changing.

"One evening he went through the 'Burial' line byline with Mrs. Flecker and myself. He had always relied greatly on his wife's taste, and I may state with absolute certainty that the only two persons who ever really influenced him in literary matters were the Oxford friend I have already mentioned and the lady whose devotion prolonged his life, and whose acute feeling for literature helped to a great extent to confirm him in his lofty ideals of artistic perfection.

"Although he never really finished the longer version of the 'Burial' which he had projected, the alterations and additions he made that evening—'Toledo-wrought neither to break nor bend ' was one of the latter—were in the mam improvements and in no way suggested that his end was so near. To me, of course, that poem must always remain intolerably sad, but, as I re-read it the other day, I asked myself whether the casual reader would feel any trace of the 'mattrass grave' on which it was written. Candidly I do not think that even the sharpest of critics would have known, if he had not been told, that half the lines were written within a month of the author's death."

His letters, as is remarked above, were generally business-like and blunt. I have found a few to myself: they are almost all about his work, with here and there a short, exclamatory eulogy of some other writer. He observes, in December 1913, that a journal which had often published him had given "The Golden Journey" "an insolent ten-line review with a batch of nincompoops"; then alternately he is better and writing copiously, or very ill and not capable of a word. In one letter he talks of writing on Balkan Politics and Italy in Albania; in another of translating some war-poetry of Paul Deroulede's.

Another time he is even thinking of "having a bang at the Cambridge Local Examination... with a whack in it at B. Shaw." Then in November 1914 he says: "I have exhausted myself writing heroic great war-poems." He might comprehensibly have been in low spirits, dying there in a dismal and deserted "health resort " among the Swiss mountains, with a continent of war-zones cutting him off from all chance of seeing friends. But he always wrote cheerfully, even when desperately ill. The French recovery filled him with enthusiasm; he watched the Near Eastern tangle with the peculiar interest of one who 'knew the peoples involved; and in one delicate and capricious piece of prose, published in a weekly in October, he recalled his own experiences of warfare. He had had glimpses of the Turco-Italian War: Italian shells over Beyrout ("Unforgettable the thunder of the guns shaking the golden blue of sky and sea while not a breath stirred the palm-trees, not a cloud moved on the swanlike snows of Lebanon") and a "scrap" with the Druses, and the smoke and distant rumble of the battle of Lemnos, "the one effort of the Turks to secure the mastery of the Ægean." These were his exciting memories:

"To think that it was with cheerful anecdotes like these that I had hoped, a white-haired elder, to impress my grandchildren! Now there's not a peasant from Picardy to Tobolsk but will cap me with tales of real and frightful tragedy. What a race of deep-eyed and thoughtful men we shall have in Europe now that all those millions have been baptized in fire!"

Then in the first week of January 1915 he died. I cannot help remembering that I first heard the news over the telephone, and that the voice which spoke was Rupert Brooke's.

J. C. SQUIRE

James Elroy Flecker – A Short Biography

James Elroy Flecker was born on 5th November 1884, in Lewisham, London to father William Hermann Flecker, an Anglican clergyman and mother Sarah (née Ducat) both of Polish Jewish origin. Both had fled to England because of persecution when they converted to Christianity.

Flecker was baptized as Herman Elroy Flecker, but later chose to use "James". He was educated at Dean Close School, Cheltenham, where his father was the headmaster, and then Uppingham School before proceeding to Trinity College, Oxford, and Gonville and Caius College, Cambridge. While at Oxford he was greatly influenced by the last years of the Aesthetic movement there under John Addington Symonds, and became a close friend of the classicist and art historian John Beazley.

At this stage Flecker does not seem to have been greatly motivated by academic study. He only achieved third-class honours in Greats in 1906. This did not set him up for a job in either government service or the academic world.

After some frustrating forays at school teaching in 1907 he attempted to enter the Levant Consular Service, more properly known as "His Majesty's Consular service in the Ottoman dominions, Persia, Greece and Morocco". The job came with a salary of £200 per annum. However, if after two years the entrant failed the examinations his bond of £500 (mainly provided by his parents) would be lost. On the positive side the standard of entrants was generally rather low as the jobs outcome was not in the exotic European and world capitals but unattractive climates or dreary oriental provincial towns.

Preparations for the Student Interpreters' examination involved two years' study at Cambridge, learning the local languages. As we know academic study was not a motivator for Flecker and the first of these two years was at best far below what he could do. He was placed 4th out of 6 candidates, with the "clever but erratic" phrase marked on his file. Now knowing that all might now be lost Flecker realised that his primary ambition of a literary and poetic career was far from being certain and a back-up plan of a secure job had to be made safe. He duly knuckled down and passed the consular examinations with first-class honours. It was now reported to the Home Office that "Mr. Flecker has recovered the ground he lost last year in a really marvellous way and deserves the highest credit for the way he has worked during the last year".

He now entered the Levant Consular Service and in June 1910 was dispatched to the Ottoman capital of Constantinople, where he was attached to the British consulate.

However, Flecker's poetry career had made progress and he was beginning to garner praise for his poetry volumes including "The Bridge of Fire" from 1907 and "The Last Generation", a short novel in 1908. Works would now follow on a regular basis. He worked slowly but with great precision and paid far more attention to his writing than his job. Unfortunately, the then dreaded tuberculosis was also making progress in him. The preliminary symptoms were already apparent, and bouts of ill health were to alternate with periods of physical well-being woven with mental euphoria and creativity. He had already spent a period in back in England in the Cotswolds convalescing at a sanitorium. These episodes would now be a feature of his life.

On the boat to Constantinople, he fell in love with a Greek woman from Athens, Hellt Skiaderessi, and married her, in the face of parental anxiety about his lowly salary and his future health prospects, in May 1911.

He seems to have performed his consular duties, when he was well, in Constantinople, Smyrna and then, after September 1911, as Vice-Consul in Beirut, in a careless and rather sloppy manner. He and Hellt were always stretched financially and required frequent subsidies from home.

His continuing examinations in Ottoman Law were not properly prepared for. Some were failed and once he was very nearly dismissed, putting the £500 bond once more in danger of being forfeited. For unknown reasons the Foreign Office in London were tolerant over this putting it down to his ongoing battle with tuberculosis and tolerant of his extended periods of leave.

Flecker began work on "Hassan" during a stay on Corfu in the summer of 1911 where he was working on his Turkish for a forthcoming consular examination and was reading various works in Turkish, including a volume of farcical tales, in one of which a simple old man, Hassan, is duped over a supposed love philtre by a Jewish magician, Zachariah. Flecker set his rendition in Baghdad rather than Turkey and began work.

Hassan too was much revised, and the final version, which was to form the basis for the acting text—Flecker was adamant that it should appear on the London stage—was not made till Autumn 1914 when he was at Davos. During its three-year gestation it went from a play with pantomime elements to a drama of human disillusionment and a climax of high tragedy. (Sadly, with the brutal intervention of World War I and the need for elaborate and expensive staging it would not debut on a London Stage until 20th September 1923, although it had premiered three months earlier in a German translation in Darmstadt.)

A visit to Damascus for Christmas 1911, a city he was always enchanted by, provided inspiration for "The Gates of Damascus", a poem it is said "marks the high point of Flecker's achievement in the oriental mood, since it combines powerful and concentrated ideas with an assured and free manipulation of the Persian-style internal and external rhymes". Flecker would also describe this as his greatest poem. In 1913 he had written a friend saying "I consider this to be my greatest poem ... It was inspired by Damascus itself by the way. I loathe the East and the Easterns, and spent all my time there dreaming of Oxford. Yet it seems, even to hardened Orientalists, that I understand".

Much of Flecker's work was based on Islamic themes and is immensely satisfying. However, Flecker himself seems to be at growing odds with them in reality often demonstrating an increasing lack of sympathy and respect to them.

As Flecker's health continued to deteriorate he now spent the last twenty months of his life in sanitoriums in Leysin and Davos. Here he carefully revised and improved all his work, usually producing more disciplined and pleasing versions of his works.

James Elroy Flecker died on 3rd January 1915, of tuberculosis, in Davos, Switzerland. His death at the age of thirty was described at the time as "unquestionably the greatest premature loss that English literature has suffered since the death of Keats".

James Elroy Flecker – A Concise Bibliography

Poetry

The Bridge of Fire (1907)
Thirty-Six Poems (1910)
Forty-Two Poems (1911)
The Golden Journey to Samarkand (1913)
The Old Ships (1915)
The Collected Poems (1916)

Novels

The Last Generation: A Story of the Future (1908)
The King of Alsander (1914)

Drama

Hassan: The Story of Hassan of Baghdad & How he Came to Make the Golden Journey to Samarkand (1922)
Incidental music to the play was written by Frederick Delius in 1920, before the play's publication, and first performed in September 1923.
Don Juan (1925)

Other

The Grecians (1910)
The Scholars' Italian Book (1911)
Collected Prose (1920)
The Letters of J.E. Flecker to Frank Savery (1926)
Some Letters from Abroad of James Elroy Flecker (1930)

www.ingramcontent.com/pod-product-compliance
Lightning Source LLC
Chambersburg PA
CBHW061446040426
42450CB00007B/1232